THE STOVE-TOP COOKBOOK

THE
STOVE-TOP
COOKBOOK

Mala Reynaud

W. H. ALLEN · LONDON · 1961

First British edition, 1961

Printed in Great Britain by
Cox and Wyman Ltd., London, Reading and Fakenham
for the publishers, W. H. Allen & Co. Ltd., Essex Street, London, WC2

To my articulate tasters, Ernie, Peter, and Pepper

CONTENTS

FOREWORD

THIS cookery book has evolved out of my reluctance to turn on the oven at any time. It is natural that during warm weather one should dislike heating up the kitchen with the oven. But with the limited storage space in my tiny city kitchen, the oven serves as a place for clumsy items, and I dislike using it at any season.

So in order to avoid confusion and frustration, and because I love to entertain, cooking on top of the cooker has become a challenge to me. As a result, I have what I think is a choice collection of workable recipes for what I call "stove-top" cooking for my family and friends.

I have been delightfully surprised to discover the many excellent dishes that can be prepared on the top of the range. A large part of my entertaining has been done with such cookery, from hors d'oeuvres to dessert. I have prepared every recipe in this book many times. I honestly believe that if the instructions are followed carefully, they are foolproof. Many of them are for dishes of other lands, but these have been adapted to ingredients available in England.

You will also find here fifty-four full-course menus planned for this type of cookery. Many, except for the vegetable course, can be prepared well ahead, leaving host or hostess unhurried, unharried, and with more time for guests. The menus are built around main dishes of meat, poultry, and fish, and are usually based upon a 6-course plan: 1-Hors d'Oeuvre, Appetizer, or

Soup; 2-Main Dish; 3-Vegetables; 4-Starchy Dish; 5-Salad; 6-Dessert. The first course, usually an hors d'oeuvre or appetizer, is meant to be served—but need not be—with a pre-dinner cocktail or *apéritif*. In several cases the salad has been omitted because of the nature of the first course or vegetable. I have chosen this menu plan because it is flexible enough to be used for both family and guests. Use them if you wish, as they stand, for guests. Omit a course or two for family, but try to retain the vegetable dish in addition to the main one for nutrition's sake.

Calorie watchers will find that suggested combinations of main dish, vegetable course, and salad can easily be converted to their special use. They will also be interested in knowing that I have pared down or eliminated dishes too heavy in calories. A minimum of fat, cream, sugar, starch, etc., is called for in these recipes (except for starchy ones *per se*) consonant with savoury food preparations. I have depended often upon the use of spices and herbs, a little wine or liqueur at times, contrasts in texture, and both contrasts and complements of flavours to add that gourmet touch to meals.

MALA REYNAUD

KITCHEN EQUIPMENT FOR
COOKING ON TOP OF THE COOKER

Ӿ　　Ӿ　　Ӿ　　Ӿ　　Ӿ　　Ӿ　　Ӿ　　Ӿ

I N an emergency, an ingenious cook with only a couple of
frying pans can, by skilful juggling and a good deal of time,
produce delightful dishes. But the household chef needs and
should find the right tools to facilitate cooking, save time, and
produce reliable results. How irritating and clumsy it is to
try to purée vegetables or fruit with a sieve and a spoon, when a
food mill, made especially for this purpose, does the job with a
few turns of the handle. Of course, you can pamper yourself
with an electric blender which purées any food in a few seconds.
But a good collection of basic "hand tools" is indispensable.

I cannot emphasize too strongly the importance, moreover, of
proper-sized pots and pans. In pot-roasting meat, for instance, a
pan too large or too light necessitates the addition of too much
liquid and also causes undesirable evaporation as the larger or
thinner surface is exposed to heat. The inevitable result: taste-
less meat. The use of a frying-pan which is too large will involve
the addition of more fat than is needed. This will be likely to
burn if no food covers it. The result is burned, hard-to-scour
yellow stains on the pan. Use a pot or pan just large enough to
hold what you want to cook in it.

1

⚡ BASIC KITCHEN EQUIPMENT

POTS AND PANS

2 frying-pans, or skillets: 6–6½ inches and 9 inches in diameter, of pre-seasoned cast iron or other heavy metal, preferably with covers

11-inch heavy metal or enamel-lined cast-iron casserole with cover

3 saucepans with covers, small, medium, and large, with frying basket for deep-fat frying

large (4- or 5-quart) pan with rack: for poached fish, steamed puddings, spaghetti

double boiler

2-cup mould with cover, for steaming

2-cup mould for refrigerator desserts

6 individual ½-cup moulds or custard cups

2- or 3-cup soufflé dish

griddle

large oblong shallow pan: to hold hot water, in which pots can be placed to keep food warm

egg poacher

TOOLS AND GADGETS

3 knives: a short paring knife for vegetables, a medium paring knife for trimming meat and poultry, and a long thin-bladed slicer for meat

potato peeler

2 pairs scissors: large for cutting poultry, tiny for snipping parsley, etc.

2 wooden mixing spoons (especially useful for lifting whole cooked poultry without piercing)

slotted or perforated serving spoon

2

spatula

measuring cup (*American—see page* 11)

set of measuring spoon (*American—see page* 11)

mixing bowls, assorted sizes

salad bowl, preferably deep rather than wide, for the safe tossing of greens

wire whisk for smooth sauces (my most-used tool)

egg beater (invest in a good one)

colander

small fine strainer

medium sieve

flour sifter

food mill

pepper mill (fresh-ground pepper adds character to cooking)

mortar and pestle, medium size

garlic press

cheese grater

graters, coarse and fine

nut chopper

chopping bowl and chopper

pastry brush: for greasing pan and griddle (get a good one so that the bristles do not fall out)

timer

✻ NICE-TO-HAVE EQUIPMENT

POTS AND PANS

electric skillet: for pot roasts, stews, fried foods (requires little or no watching; good for use at the table and outdoors)

deep fat fryer and basket

earthenware casserole (use only with asbestos pad; pour no cold liquids into it while hot)

cast-iron frying-pan reserved for omelet, 10-inch diameter for 3
    or 4 eggs
pressure cooker (especially good for dried beans, which it cooks
    in about 20 minutes)
electric griddle (some come with hot storage tray)
Swedish plett pan: a cast-iron griddle with several rounded
    grooves for making tiny pancakes for desserts and hors
    d'oeuvres, and toasting small amounts of biscuits

TOOLS AND GADGETS

electric hand beater
meat grinder
electric blender
candle warmer: for buffet service
electric hot tray or warmer (the best possible thing for keeping
    food warm)

HERBS, SPICES, AND
OTHER SEASONING

THE brilliant French epicure, de la Reynière, referred to seasonings as the "hidden soul of cooking". Used sparingly and with knowledge, they should produce a subtle combination of flavours without destroying the natural taste of the food. When a pleasing dish evokes a complimentary "How ever did you season it?" you have achieved the proper blend.

Buy seasonings of good quality and in small amounts. Keep them tightly covered to prevent deterioration. It is not necessary to have a stock of every seasoning. If I were limited to five herbs, I would choose parsley, tarragon, thyme, oregano, and garlic. Could I add several more, chives, bay leaf, basil, dill, and rosemary would be included. By all means use fresh herbs when they are available. Besides parsley, good shops occasionally carry chives and dill. It is best not to wash fresh herbs. If you must cleanse them, wrap enough for immediate use in a cloth or paper towel, dampen it slightly, and press with your fingers. Any grit or sand will adhere to the wrapping. To release the full strength of fresh herbs, mince them finely with a tiny pair of scissors; if they are dried, powder them between the fingers. One tablespoon of the fresh is equivalent to about ¾ teaspoon of the dried.

Don't be afraid to experiment. Try a seasoning singly, or two or three together in a dish. Start with a pinch and gradually increase the amount until you reach the desired result. Below are lists of some herbs, spices, etc., together with foods they complement or enhance. Use them as a guide when you experiment.

✄ HERBS

PARSLEY: a garnish for boiled lobster, sautéed fish and chicken, boiled potatoes, asparagus, aubergine, carrots, mushrooms, dried beans, lentils; use in meat balls and loaf, stews, sauces, soups, stuffing, court bouillon, scrambled eggs, omelet—in fact, practically everything except desserts.

TARRAGON: chicken, lobster, cold salmon and other fish, scrambled and poached eggs, omelets, tomatoes, tartar sauce, salads and salad dressings, stuffing, aspic.

THYME: veal, beef stews and pot roasts, minced-beef dishes, fish, fish and clam chowders, tomatoes, stuffing, sauces; thyme and bay are often used together.

OREGANO: minced-beef dishes, beef stews and pot roasts, lamb and chicken stews, tomato sauce and salad, potato salad, baby marrows, kidney beans, lentils, stuffing; and marinated aubergine, mushrooms, and carrots; can be used in place of sweet marjoram in many dishes.

GARLIC: shrimp, fish, liver, meats, poultry, game, salad dressing, soups, sauces, sautéed cabbage, aubergine, broccoli, baby marrows, squash, stuffed tomatoes, heated French or Italian bread.

CHIVES: lamb, dried beans, tomatoes, eggs, cream cheese, butter sauces, salads, potatoes, Vichyssoise, fish; used chiefly as a garnish and usually added at the last moment.

BAY LEAF: mussels and other sea food, fish and meat stews, boiled ham, meat sauces and gravies, pea soup.

BASIL: all tomato dishes (including sauces), meatloaf, aubergine.

DILL: cucumber, tomato and potato salads, shrimp, lobster, fish

6

and fish sauces, boiled lamb sauce, cucumber pickle; use the fresh leaves liberally, the seed or salt sparingly.

ROSEMARY: lamb, pork, veal, chicken, peas.

CHERVIL: garnish for potato and cauliflower salads, consommé, pea and dried-bean soups, potato soups, separately or with parsley and tarragon to garnish sautéed chicken.

MARJORAM: lamb, pork, ground meats, game, Brussels sprouts, cauliflower, cabbage, aubergine, broccoli.

SAGE: pork, stuffings.

✸ SPICES

SALT: to be used carefully with fish, cheese, and wine dishes; use a pinch in cooked fruit dishes to bring out the flavour.

BLACK PEPPER: preferably ground in your own pepper mill; essential in salads. Use white pepper or cayenne in white sauces or light dishes where colour is important.

SUGAR: to be used in minute quantities for browning beef and lamb; with turnips, peas, carrots, cabbage, corn, sweet potatoes.

NUTMEG: spinach, carrots, potato and shrimp soups, custard, pumpkin.

PAPRIKA: goulash and other stews, sauces, soups, as a garnish for stuffed eggs, celery.

CURRY: sauces, soups, shellfish, fish, poultry, lamb, beef, veal, lentils, vegetables, rice, hard-boiled eggs.

CAYENNE: cream sauces, lobster, oyster, fish dishes.

SAFFRON: rice, fish, and fish soups; easiest to use in powder form.

GINGER and CINNAMON: fruits, puddings, other desserts.

MUSTARD: the dry where zip without colour is wanted; for variety, try Dijon mustard and Bavarian-style mustard made with Moselle wine.

❄ OTHER FLAVOURINGS

OLIVE OIL: not exactly a flavouring, but it does flavour food; try to use a high-quality oil.

VINEGAR: can make or break your salad; use a mild, good wine vinegar.

VANILLA: to be used in the bean to flavour dessert syrups; use vanilla sugar where sugar plus extract is called for. (Vanilla sugar: drop a 2- or 3-inch piece of bean, minced, into a 1- to 2-pound glass jar of sugar with a tight cover; use after 2 or 3 days as you need it.)

USING WINE
TO FLAVOUR FOOD

※　　※　　※　　※　　※　　※　　※　　※

WINE in food provides aroma, not alcohol. The latter is evaporated in cooking, and only the delicious perfume remains. Virtually all classes of food benefit from the judicious use of a little wine. When correctly used, it never dominates a dish, but accents its characteristic flavour, combining subtly with the food and the other seasonings. As a marinade, with oil, herbs, and spices, it softens tough cuts of meat.

In France, where cooking with wine is a casual and well-understood practice, remnants of table wine are used. There is no such thing as a cooking wine. Use a good table wine, not necessarily imported or costly. The oft-repeated generality that red wine goes with dark meat and white with light meat and fish, is worth remembering. In French and Spanish cuisine, however, there are many exceptions where the liquors of the locality are used, including beer, cider, vermouth, sherry, etc. Even fish, with its long-established affinity for white wine, is occasionally prepared with red. Pork and veal can be treated with white or red; lobster with white wine, or sherry.

Port, sweet white wine, and liqueurs are mainly confined to desserts. Use only minute amounts of liqueurs. Too little is far

9

better than too much. If the dessert has a distinct liqueur perfume, you've overdone it. For flaming foods and for flavouring fruits and other desserts, brandy is almost indispensable.

Observe these rules when cooking with wine:

1. Cover foods closely to keep in aroma.
2. Be sparing with sherry. It is a potent flavouring; 2 tablespoons equal about ½ cup of red or white wine.
3. Watch wine when it is used with cream or milk. To prevent curdling, simmer the wine well first; add cream or milk away from heat. Reheat slowly if necessary, but without permitting it to boil.
4. When preparing a quick dish, reduce the added wine by half, by fast boiling, to expel alcohol and concentrate flavour.
5. Keep wine away from egg dishes generally.

The wine-food groups below are meant to inspire you. Don't be awed by wine as a cooking ingredient. Be daring in intention but conservative in its use.

RED WINE
    beef, game, pork, red cabbage, lamb,
    gravies and sauces, duck, marinade for meats

SHERRY
    lobster, duck, veal, mushrooms, beef,
    jellied consommé, ham, fish sauces, lamb,
    dessert sauces, chicken

WHITE WINE
    fish and shellfish, sausage, veal, mushrooms, ham,
    white cabbage, pork, sauerkraut, potato salad, lamb,
    fish soup and sauces, chicken, onion soup, rabbit, fruit

PORT
    beef, duck, game, ox tongue, fruit

VERMOUTH
    beef balls, beef stew

HOW TO USE
THE RECIPES

I RECOMMEND reading the recipe through first to get the general idea. Use American standard measuring cup and spoons as all recipes in this book are based on them. An American measuring cup holds approximately 8 fluid ounces (three eighths of a pint). An American measuring tablespoon holds $\frac{1}{2}$ fluid ounce or about $\frac{1}{4}$ oz. flour. All measurements should be level unless otherwise specified. If at the beginning you can gather together near your working area all the ingredients and tools you will need, much time and many steps will be saved. Try not to make a substitution for any ingredient given; it may be the one that gives the dish its character. Preparation time, which can only be approximate, is given for almost all the recipes. In the menus, dishes for which recipes are included in this book are listed in small capital letters.

MEAT AND POULTRY
MAIN DISHES

B E sure to buy the best quality meat for steaks, chops, and roasts. The less tender grades, however, are still nutritious, and can be successfully cooked by means of moist and slow heat.

Since, by its very nature, meat cooked on the top of the stove must be sautéed or fried, stewed or pot-roasted, the use of fat should be understood. In browning meats for stews or roasts, a minimum amount of fat should be used. The browning process should be quick in order to close the pores of the meat, seal in the juices, and thus preserve flavour and moisture. Butter, or better still, a mixture of oil and butter, is good for this job. The special flavour of butter plus the higher boiling point of oil makes this a fine combination. If the meat has fat of its own, use that.

After the meat has been browned, the fat should be poured off unless you are otherwise directed. Generally speaking, some liquid should then be poured into the pan to be mixed with the meat particles left there, and the resulting gravy added to the meat. Midway during cooking or immediately after, most of the fat should be skimmed off. Stews, which seem to improve the second day, may be cooked a day ahead (except for the vegetables) and refrigerated. The congealed fat can then be lifted out, although a stew is at its best when a little fat is left in.

Too much liquid produces poor results in these dishes. The less liquid, the more taste. In the savoury Brisket of Beef Pot Roast, no liquid at all is used; the onions supply plenty of juice. Since pots and pans vary so much in size and shape, it is impossible to prescribe exact amounts of liquid. Use a pot that fits the meat, and let the liquid reach about one third but not more than one half the height of the meat. You will find that the liquid seems to increase rather than decrease during the first hour of cooking.

The modern broiler-fryer chicken (2 to $3\frac{1}{2}$ pounds) can be prepared either way, as the name suggests. I prefer either a fryer or a roasting chicken ($3\frac{1}{2}$ to $4\frac{1}{2}$ pounds) for stewing. A hen weighing between 5 and 8 pounds is fine for soup and fricassée too. Bear in mind that a $4\frac{1}{2}$-pound duck, with its large proportion of fat, offers fewer servings than a $3\frac{1}{2}$-pound chicken.

If freshly killed poultry is available, you are indeed fortunate. Fresh or frozen, even dressed poultry requires some preliminary preparation. Remove the pin feathers with tweezers or a small knife. Singe the tiny hairs by rotating the bird over a burner. Then hold it under cold running water, rinse out the inside quickly, and dry. Rub the outside with half a lemon, squeezing it as you rub. If the bird is purchased in parts, remove the pin feathers and hairs as above. Don't rinse, but rub each part all over with a cut lemon.

❧ CARBONNADE FLAMANDE · Flemish Stew

SERVES 4 · 2½ TO 3 HOURS

2 *pounds boneless beef chuck,* *cubed*	2 *tablespoons butter*
1 *tablespoon flour*	1 *cup beer*
½ *teaspoon salt*	1 *clove garlic, crushed*
¼ *teaspoon pepper*	½ *teaspoon sugar*
2 *large onions*	½ *teaspoon vinegar*

1. Combine flour, salt, and pepper in a small paper bag. Shake meat cubes in mixture and coat all over.

2. Slice onions. Sauté them briefly in 1 tablespoon of hot butter in a casserole. Remove onions. Add other tablespoon of butter and brown meat quickly. Pour off any remaining fat.

3. Add onions, beer, crushed garlic, and sugar. Bring to a boil. Cover and simmer until tender, about 2 to 2½ hours.

4. Strain sauce into another pan. Return meat to sauce. Add vinegar and mix. Taste to correct seasoning.

5. Serve hot on a platter with some of the sauce over the meat. Arrange chive potatoes in the centre.

A popular Belgian family dish; fine for company too. A glass of beer to drink with it is perfect.

Suggested Menu: LIVER PÂTÉ; CARBONNADE FLAMANDE; CHIVE POTATOES; GLAZED CARROT STICKS; endive, chicory, and beet salad, CREAMY SALAD DRESSING; TINNED PEARS IN SAUTERNE.

✄ BEEF BOURGUIGNONNE

SERVES 4 · 2¾ HOURS

2 *pounds round steak, cubed*	⅛ *teaspoon pepper*
2 *shallots or 1 small onion*	*Good pinch thyme*
2 *tablespoons parsley*	1 *bay leaf*
4 *slices bacon*	4 *medium-sized carrots*
3 *tablespoons brandy*	8 *small white onions*
1 *tablespoon flour*	¼ *pound fresh mushrooms*
½ *cup hot beef stock*	*(or small tin whole*
1 *cup dry red wine*	*mushrooms)*
½ *teaspoon salt*	2 *tablespoons butter*

1. Chop shallots or onion, and parsley. Dice bacon into a skillet and fry to just below point of crispness. Transfer bacon to a casserole which can be used over the ring on the top of the cooker. Sear beef quickly in bacon fat in skillet. Arrange over bacon in casserole. Cook shallots or onion 2 or 3 minutes in skillet and add to beef with half the parsley.

2. Pour brandy over beef, and touch a lighted match to it. Let it blaze a few seconds, and, when it is about to die down, cover quickly.

3. Pour off all but 1 tablespoon of fat from skillet. Blend in flour away from heat. Add stock wine, and liquor from tinned mushrooms, if you are using them. Return to fire, stir with a wire whisk, and bring to a boil. Pour sauce over beef. Add salt, pepper, thyme, and bay leaf. Simmer covered 1¾ hours, Remove bay leaf.

4. Cut carrots in half crosswise. Round off corners and shape like small chubby carrots. Peel onions. Halve fresh mushrooms if you are using them. Toss all three vegetables (except tinned mushrooms, if you are using them) in hot butter in skillet 3 or 4 minutes. Add to casserole. Cook over low heat until meat and vegetables are done, about 25 minutes. (Add tinned mushrooms after tossing in hot butter, 5 minutes before other vegetables are done.)

16

5. Serve from casserole or arrange on a hot platter, vegetables in the centre, surrounded by meat cubes. Sprinkle with remaining parsley.

Suggested Menu: COLD SALMON, MAYONNAISE CAPER SAUCE; BEEF BOURGUIGNONNE; carrots, onions, mushrooms, cooked in stew; NOODLE PUDDING KEREKES; GREEN AND RED PEPPER SALAD; Gruyère, Brie, cottage cheese, with bowl of fruit (see CHEESE AND FRUIT FOR DESSERT).

HUNGARIAN BEEF GOULASH

SERVES 4 · ABOUT 3 HOURS

2 *pounds lean beef chuck or*	2 *tablespoons oil*
rump, cubed	1 *tablespoon paprika*
2 *large onions*	$\frac{1}{2}$ *cup chicken broth*
1 *green pepper*	1 *teaspoon salt*

1. Remove all fat from meat. Wipe with a damp paper towel or cloth. Chop onions and green pepper finely.
2. Heat 1 tablespoon of oil in a skillet over moderate heat. Brown beef quickly. Transfer to a pot.
3. Add other tablespoon of oil. Brown onions lightly. Stir in paprika. Cook $\frac{1}{2}$ minute. Add broth, scrape pan, and stir to blend in meat particles. Add to meat in pot.
4. Add uncooked green pepper and salt. Cover and simmer until fork tender, about $2\frac{1}{2}$ hours.

An easy, savoury dish which never fails. Like all stews, it seems to taste better the next day. Try this recipe also with short ribs of beef. Remove as much fat as you can from ribs before cooking, skim off more fat as ribs cook, and skim again before serving.

Suggested Menu: celery stuffed with GUACAMOLE; HUNGARIAN BEEF GOULASH; green tomato and sweet red pepper pickles; POTATO PUDDING; buttered green beans, wedges of lettuce,

CREAMY SALAD DRESSING WITH KETCHUP; PRUNES AND KUM-
QUATS AU COGNAC.

✻ BEEF STEW BALDWIN PLACE

SERVES 4 · 3 HOURS

1½ to 2 *pounds lean beef,* *cubed*	2½ *tablespoons olive oil*
1 *green pepper*	¼ *cup dry red wine*
1 *large ripe tomato*	¼ *cup water*
1 *medium-sized onion*	1 *chicken bouillon cube*
1 *clove garlic*	¼ *teaspoon thyme*
2 *tablespoons flour*	¼ *teaspoon basil*
½ *teaspoon salt*	4 *small carrots*
¼ *teaspoon paprika*	4 *small potatoes*
½ *teaspoon chili powder*	1 *tablespoon chopped parsley*

1. Wipe beef with a damp cloth or paper towel, core and slice green pepper in rings. Skin and cube tomato. Slice onion thinly and mince garlic.

2. Combine flour, salt, paprika, and chili powder in a paper bag. Shake meat in mixture to coat.

3. Heat oil in a casserole over medium heat. Brown meat quickly on all sides. Add green pepper, onion, and garlic, and cook 3 minutes. Add wine. Loosen meat particles on bottom of pan and mix. Cook, covered for 10 minutes. Add water, bouillon cube, and tomato, and bring to boil. Mix with spoon to blend bouillon cube with liquid. Add thyme and basil. Lower heat and simmer 2 hours.

4. Scrape carrots and peel potatoes. Cook ½ hour with meat. Chop parsley.

5. Place meat cubes in deep dish. Arrange vegetables around them. Cover with some of the sauce and garnish with parsley. Pass remainder of sauce.

18

For a buffet dinner on a winter evening, this spicy stew is perfect.

Suggested Menu: citrus fruit-juice cocktail au Cointreau; BEEF STEW BALDWIN PLACE; potatoes and carrots from stew; COLE SLAW, FRENCH DRESSING; PARADISE PUDDING, CRANBERRY-APPLE SAUCE.

⚶ BEEF CREOLE WITH KIDNEY BEANS
SERVES 4 · 2¼ TO 2¾ HOURS

2 *pounds beef rump or chuck,*	½ *teaspoon salt*
cubed	⅛ *teaspoon pepper*
2 *large onions*	1 *tablespoon chili powder*
1 *tin tomatoes*	1 *pound tinned kidney beans*
4 *slices bacon*	½ *teaspoon oregano*

1. Wipe meat with damp paper towel.
2. Dice onions. Drain tomatoes and save liquid for some other use.
3. Place bacon on bottom of a casserole or pan. Top with beef. Then with onions, tomatoes, salt, pepper, and chili powder. Cover and simmer 2 to 2½ hours. Crush tomatoes once or twice with back of spoon. Stir occasionally.
4. Drain beans. Add a little bean liquid if sauce is too thick. When meat is tender, stir in beans, turn up heat somewhat and cook until beans are heated through and blended with sauce.
5. Remove beef to a hot platter. Border with beans. Sprinkle oregano, powdering it with fingers, over beans. Pass sauce.

This chili is not too hot nor timidly mild. As it cooks, the chili flavour mellows rather than sharpens.

Suggested Menu: carrot and celery curls (see RAW VEGETABLE PLATTER), green olives; BEEF CREOLE WITH KIDNEY BEANS; BOILED RICE or RICE PILAF; GREEN AND RED PEPPER SALAD; AMBROSIA.

✄ POT-ROASTED SKILLET STEAK

SERVES 4 · 2 HOURS

A 2-*pound slice top sirloin of beef*	1 *tablespoon butter*
2 *carrots*	1 *cup hot beef stock*
½ *large green pepper*	1 *heaped tablespoon tomato paste*
1 *large onion*	4 *to* 6 *potatoes*
1 *clove garlic*	*Salt to taste*
1½ *tablespoons flour*	⅛ *teaspoon pepper*
1 *tablespoon oil*	¼ *cup port wine*

1. Chop carrots and green pepper very finely. Place in the bottom of a shallow casserole. Chop onion finely and mince garlic; set aside. Pound flour into meat on both sides with the edge of a plate or a mallet.
2. Heat oil and butter in a skillet; brown beef quickly on both sides. Remove to casserole. Add onion and garlic to skillet and brown lightly. Drain off any fat in pan. Pour in stock. Mix in tomato paste. Scrape skillet and pour contents over beef. Bring to boil. Simmer covered 1 hour, basting occasionally.
3. Peel potatoes. Turn meat. Add salt to taste, pepper, and potatoes. Simmer until potatoes and meat are done, about ¾ hour. Blend in wine. Cook 2 minutes more. Serve.

The carrots, green pepper, and port impart a special delicious flavour to the beef.

Suggested Menu: ARTICHOKES, RUSSIAN DRESSING; POT-ROASTED SKILLET STEAK; potatoes cooked with steak; CELERY SALAD on tomato slices; sliced sugared strawberries in kirsch, vanilla ice cream (SEE FRUIT FLAVOURED WITH LIQUEUR).

⚜ BRISKET OF BEEF POT ROAST

SERVES 6 TO 8 · 4¼ HOURS

3 *or* 4 *pounds brisket of beef,*	1 *bay leaf*
first cut	2 *whole allspice*
3 *large onions*	*Flour*
1½ *teaspoons salt*	1 *tablespoon chopped parsley*
¼ *teaspoon pepper*	

1. Slice onions thinly, and set aside. Trim off part of beef fat. Wipe roast with damp paper towel.
2. Place beef in an enamel-lined cast-iron casserole or heavy saucepan over moderate heat. Let brown in its own fat on all sides, seasoning with salt and pepper as it browns. Remove beef. Pour off all fat. Add onions, separated into rings. Lay meat over them. Add bay leaf, crushed, and allspice. Cover and simmer 1 hour. Turn brisket over. Simmer 2 hours, basting occasionally. Remove meat to platter.
3. Strain broth; measure and return it to pot. Blend flour (1⅓ tablespoons for each cup of broth) with as little cold water as possible. Stir into broth. Bring to boil; add seasoning if needed; lower flame. Replace beef in gravy and simmer 1 hour or until tender. Chop parsley.
4. Slice meat thinly. Arrange on hot platter, slices overlapping. Cover partially with sauce. Garnish with chopped parsley.

This cut of beef requires long, slow cooking and slices beautifully. It is a dish full of flavour, being cooked without any water.

Suggested Menu: TUNA-PARMESAN PÂTÉ in tomato cups; BRISKET OF BEEF; kosher-style cucumber pickles; KASHA; steamed buttered cauliflower; COLE SLAW, FRENCH DRESSING; ORANGE COMPÔTE.

✄ POT-AU-FEU

SERVES 8 TO 10 · 4½ HOURS

3 *pounds brisket of beef, most but not all fat removed*
1 *small stewing chicken, whole or split in half*
1 *or 2 marrow bones*
4 *or 5 quarts cold water*
1 *large tomato*
2 *teaspoons salt*
¼ *teaspoon pepper*
2 *onions, each stuck with 1 clove*
2 *parsnips*
4 *sprigs parsley*
1 *large bay leaf*
1 *clove garlic*
4 *or 5 small carrots*
2 *small white turnips*
6 *leeks, white and light green part only*
1 *cup celery*
1 *cup potato (optional)*
2 *small white cabbages (optional)*
2 *tablespoons butter*
Freshly ground black pepper
Coarse salt
Paprika (optional)

1. Rinse off quickly meat, chicken, and bones. Place in a large deep pot with water to cover. Chop tomato. Add with salt and pepper and bring to boil. Simmer ½ hour.

2. Prepare onions and parsnips and add whole with parsley, bay, and garlic. Simmer 3 hours.

3. Remove beef, chicken, and bones. Put broth through fine strainer. Let cool sufficiently to remove accumulated fat.

4. While broth cools, scrape carrots; peel and halve turnips; prepare leeks; dice celery and potato (optional). Add to broth from which fat has been removed. Return meat, chicken, and bones to pot. Bring to boil and simmer about 45 minutes or until vegetables are done. Correct seasoning.

5. (Omit this step if you don't want cabbage) Rinse and quarter cabbages. Cook in separate pan with a little broth from pot-au-feu. Cook uncovered about 15 minutes until crisply tender. Baste with broth once or twice. Drain and toss in butter. Sprinkle with pepper.

22

6. Remove beef, chicken, bones, turnips, leeks. Remove marrow from bones or if missing, fish up from soup and slice. Slice beef. Skin chicken and slice. Arrange on hot platter, trimmed with carrots, turnips, and leeks. Keep warm.

7. Serve broth with its diced vegetables and marrow slices from soup tureen. Offer toasted French bread, or plain biscuits. Sprinkle a little broth over meat on platter. Pass pepper mill and coarse salt (kosher salt), or HORSERADISH SAUCE. Serve cabbage, lightly dusted with paprika, in separate dish.

⅍ HORSERADISH SAUCE

SERVES 4 TO 6 · 5 MINUTES

1 *cup hot beef broth*	2 *to 3 tablespoons prepared*
1½ *tablespoons beef fat or*	*horseradish, drained*
butter	*Salt and pepper*
1½ *tablespoons flour*	

1. Have broth ready.

2. Melt fat or butter over moderate-slow heat. Add flour away from heat, stirring with a wire whisk until sauce is blended.

3. Return to heat and slowly add broth. Use whisk to stir until sauce comes to boil. Remove from heat. Stir in horseradish.

4. Season with salt and pepper to taste.

Omit potato from pot-au-feu for a very clear soup; for maximum taste, use a minimum of water. The brisket is a firm, tightly textured cut that slices beautifully. Leftover beef or chicken may be used in a curry dish (see QUICK CHICKEN CURRY) or in CHICKEN ENCHILADAS.

Suggested Menu: beef-vegetable broth from POT-AU-FEU; sliced beef and chicken from POT-AU-FEU, HORSERADISH SAUCE; kosher-style pickles; POT-AU-FEU vegetables; salad of beets julienne, CREAMY SALAD DRESSING; tinned greengages with ginger (see MORE WAYS WITH FRUIT).

✄ SAVOURY POT ROAST

SERVES 6 TO 8 · 3½ hours

3 *pounds bottom round, boneless chuck, or cross rib roast*
1 *teaspoon salt*
1 *onion*
2 *thin slices lemon*
2 *tablespoons minced parsley*
2½ *cups (tinned) tomatoes*
½ *cup beef or chicken broth*
1 *teaspoon brown sugar*
1 *bay leaf*
½ *teaspoon celery salt*
½ *teaspoon thyme*
¼ *teaspoon black pepper*
½ *cup dry red wine*
1½ *tablespoons flour mixed with 3 tablespoons cold water*

1. Sprinkle salt on the bottom of a large pot. Place pot over moderate heat. Brown meat quickly on all sides, and remove from pot.

2. Slice onion and lemon. Mince parsley. Add to pot with tomatoes and their juice, and broth. Stir and scrape well to blend with meat particles left in pot. Add all other ingredients except wine and flour mixture. Bring to a boil. Return roast to pot. Simmer covered about 3 hours or until tender. As liquid cooks down, add wine a little at a time until all of it has been added.

3. Place roast on platter and strain sauce. Remove fat from top. Correct seasoning. Thicken sauce if desired by stirring in flour mixture. Bring to boil, stirring constantly. Return meat to pot and let simmer 10 minutes. Slice and serve.

24

Reserve this dish for habitual late-comers. Extra cooking or reheating cannot spoil it.

Suggested Menu: sherried grapefruit; SAVOURY POT ROAST; PO-TATO PANCAKES; STEAMED CHOPPED BROCCOLI; fennel and red radish salad, FRENCH DRESSING; APRICOT-GLAZED APPLES.

⚓ BEEF STROGANOFF

SERVES 4 · 40 MINUTES

1 *pound beef fillet*	1 *teaspoon tomato paste*
1 *small onion*	1 *tablespoon oil*
1 *tablespoon chopped parsley*	4 *tablespoons sour cream*
3 *tablespoons butter*	*Salt to taste*
1 *tablespoon flour*	⅛ *teaspoon pepper*
1 *cup beef bouillon*	

1. Wipe meat with a damp cloth.
2. Cut beef into thin finger-length strips. Mince onion. Chop parsley.
3. Melt 1 tablespoon butter in a small pan. Blend in flour until smooth. Add bouillon gradually, stirring constantly. Bring to a boil. Stir in tomato paste and blend well. Let sauce simmer.
4. Heat oil and 2 tablespoons butter in a skillet. Lightly brown beef and onion. Pour sauce over and stir. Simmer 15 minutes. Just before serving, add sour cream, a little at a time, and let it heat slowly without boiling. Add salt if necessary and pepper.
5. Place beef with sauce on a serving dish. Sprinkle it with parsley.

Sirloin steak may be used instead of the fillet, but let it simmer in sauce longer, until tender.

Suggested Menu: CHILLED BORSCHT; BEEF STROGANOFF; RICE PILAF WITH MUSHROOMS; ZUCCHINI PATTIES; cucumber and tomato salad, FRENCH DRESSING with chopped dill; CHERRIES JUBILEE.

✄ BEEF FRICADELLES

SERVES 4 · 50 MINUTES

5 *slices fresh white bread,*	¼ *teaspoon paprika*
crusts removed	*Good pinch nutmeg*
¾ *cup milk*	*Good pinch cayenne*
1 *small onion*	¼ *cup dry white wine*
¼ *pound mushrooms*	¾ *tablespoon potato starch*
1 *teaspoon lemon juice*	— *or potato flour*
3 *tablespoons butter*	1 *teaspoon tomato paste*
¾ *pound ground raw beef,*	1½ *cups cold water*
chuck or round	1 *chicken bouillon cube*
2 *eggs*	1 *tablespoon currant or*
1 *teaspoon salt*	*raspberry jelly*
¼ *teaspoon pepper*	1 *bay leaf*
	1 *tablespoon chopped parsley*

1. Soak bread in milk in a large bowl. Mince onion. Chop mushrooms and sprinkle with lemon juice.

2. Melt 1 tablespoon butter slowly in a small pan. Sauté onion for 2 minutes. Add onion, meat, eggs, seasonings (except bay leaf) to bread and milk. Work all with fork until smooth. The mixture will be soft.

3. In a larger skillet melt 1 tablespoon of butter over medium-low heat. Shape mixture into small balls or patties and brown quickly on both sides. A nice crust should form. If mixture is too soft to handle, dip fingers into cold water and shape.

4. Pour wine over meat balls. Remove them to a plate.

5. Put remaining tablespoon of butter in skillet. Cook mushrooms 2 or 3 minutes. Blend in potato starch and tomato paste. Add water and bring to boil, stirring constantly. Add bouillon cube, jelly, and bay leaf, and crush cube with back of spoon to dissolve. Re-adjust seasoning if necessary. Return patties to sauce and simmer 20 minutes.

26

6. Arrange on a platter with some of the sauce. Sprinkle with parsley.

These meat balls are delicate and surprisingly good. This recipe makes about 24 walnut-sized balls. They may be used as an appetizer or hors d'oeuvre.

Suggested Menu: tuna-stuffed tomato slices; BEEF FRICADELLES; LYONNAISE POTATOES; CAULIFLOWER SALAD; chilled ZABAIONE.

BEEF CABBAGE ROLLS

SERVES 4 TO 6 · 1½ HOURS

2 *cups boiling stock*	*Pinch nutmeg*
1 *large white cabbage*	*Pinch cayenne*
3 *to* 4 *tablespoons tomato*	2 *tablespoons whole pine nuts*
paste	(*pignoli*), *or any other nuts,*
1 *small onion*	*slivered*
2 *tablespoons minced parsley*	1 *medium onion*
1 *tablespoon butter*	1 *tablespoon brown sugar*
1 *pound raw ground beef*	¼ *to* ½ *teaspoon lemon*
1 *cup cooked rice*	*juice, if needed*
1 *teaspoon salt*	*Paprika*
⅛ *teaspoon thyme*	

1. Bring chicken stock to boil in a large saucepan. Wash cabbage well. Place in stock. Cover and let steam over moderate heat 5 minutes. Remove cabbage. Add tomato paste and blend with stock. Turn off heat.

2. Carefully remove 12 leaves from cabbage. Reserve with remaining cabbage.

3. Mince small onion and parsley. Melt butter over moderate heat in a skillet. When it is hot, cook onion and beef until red colour leaves beef. Add parsley, rice, salt, thyme, nutmeg, cayenne, and nuts. Mix lightly.

27

4. Place large spoonful of meat mixture on each cabbage leaf. If leaf is too small, combine with another. Fold the two opposite ends over filling. Roll up and fasten securely with toothpick.

5. Slice medium-sized onion. Lay several extra cabbage leaves on bottom of saucepan. Top with sliced onion. Carefully lower rolls into stock. Bring to a boil. Simmer, covered, 1 hour. Baste 3 or 4 times.

6. Add sugar. Cook 1 minute. Taste sauce; it may need a little more salt or sugar or even a little lemon juice. Place rolls on a serving dish with a little sauce. Dust with paprika.

These rolls seem to taste even better the next day. You may vary the sauce by the addition of some raisins or a pinch of caraway seeds.

Suggested Menu: AVOCADO-STUFFED EGGS; BEEF CABBAGE ROLLS; buttered Frenched green beans; SHREDDED BABY MARROW WITH SOUR CREAM; guava jelly and cream cheese with plain cracker biscuits (see CHEESE AND FRUIT FOR DESSERT).

⅄ MEAT BALLS IN MUSHROOM SAUCE

SERVES 4 · 35 MINUTES

1 *pound beef round or chuck, ground*	1 *tablespoon grated Parmesan cheese*
2 *slices white or rye bread*	⅛ *teaspoon pepper*
1 *tablespoon minced onion*	1 *egg yolk, unbeaten*
1 *tablespoon minced parsley*	½ *teaspoon salt*
1 *tablespoon minced green pepper*	1 *small tin (1 cup) tomato sauce with mushrooms*

1. Remove crusts and soak bread in a little cold water. Prepare onion, parsley, and green pepper.

2. Combine in a large bowl the meat, onion, parsley, green pepper, cheese, pepper, and bread squeezed dry. Mix well with

28

hand. Drop egg yolk over mixture. Mix in with a fork. Shape mixture into small balls.

3. Sprinkle salt evenly on the bottom of a large skillet and heat over medium heat. Brown meat balls quickly on both sides. Pour off any fat in pan. Add mushroom sauce. Bring to a boil. Cover and cook slowly 20 minutes or longer.

A very tasty and quick dish.

Suggested Menu: ANCHOVY AND PIMENTO SALAD; MEAT BALLS IN MUSHROOM SAUCE; boiled buttered spaghetti with Parmesan cheese; BROCCOLI SAUTÉ; MOCHA PARFAIT PIE.

✢ PAN-BROILED HAMBURGERS

SERVES 3 OR 4 · 25 MINUTES

1 *pound beef chuck, round, or sirloin, ground*	$\frac{1}{8}$ *to* $\frac{1}{4}$ *teaspoon black pepper*
1 *slice bread, crusts removed*	1 *tablespoon chopped onion*
1 *small onion*	3 *tablespoons red or white wine*
1 *tablespoon chopped green pepper*	1 *tablespoon Worcester Sauce*
2 *tablespoons chopped parsley*	1$\frac{1}{2}$ *tablespoons butter*
1 *egg yolk, unbeaten*	$\frac{1}{2}$ *teaspoon salt*

1. Soak bread in a little cold water. When it is soft, squeeze it dry. Grate whole small onion coarsely. Chop green pepper and parsley. Reserve half the parsley and combine these four ingredients with beef, egg yolk, and pepper. Work with hand to blend well together. Shape into 3 or 4 patties.

2. Have ready the tablespoon of chopped onion and remaining parsley, the wine, Worcester Sauce, butter, and a warm serving dish.

3. Sprinkle salt evenly on the bottom of a skillet. Heat over moderately hot flame. Don't shake pan, or salt will slide over to one spot. Brown patties quickly on both sides. If they are not cooked through enough, cover and cook a few more minutes. Remove them to warm serving dish.

4. If skillet is very hot, hold it about 2 inches from heat to prevent undesirable evaporation, and add wine, Worcester Sauce, parsley, and onion. Swirl with spatula quickly to collect meat particles, and mix with drippings. Add butter, let melt, and stir once. Serve immediately over hamburgers.

A simple dish but always a treat.

Suggested Menu: HOT BORSCHT; PAN-BROILED HAMBURGERS; SKILLET POTATOES; GREEN BUTTERED CABBAGE; MARINATED RED ONIONS AND TOMATOES; pistachio ice cream with pineapple topping (see MORE WAYS WITH FRUIT).

⅍ FRESH BEEF TONGUE CREOLE

SERVES 4 TO 6 · 2½ TO 3½ HOURS

1 *fresh beef tongue*	1 *clove garlic (optional)*
1 *large onion*	2 *tablespoons butter or oil*
2 *ribs celery with leaves*	2 *tablespoons flour*
2 *carrots*	½ *cup tomato juice*
1 *teaspoon salt*	2 *teaspoons vinegar*
6 *peppercorns*	1 *teaspoon chili powder*
2 *tablespoons chopped onion*	1 *tablespoon brown sugar*
1 *small green pepper*	

1. Slice onion, celery, and carrots. Place with tongue, salt, and peppercorns in a pan with boiling water to cover. Bring to a boil and simmer 2 to 3 hours.

2. Drain, reserving 1 cup of stock. Skin and remove root. Slice medium-thick.

30

3. Chop onion, green pepper, and garlic. Sauté in hot butter or oil 5 minutes. Blend in flour. Add juice, stock, and vinegar away from heat, stirring. Return to heat and whisk until smooth and boiling. Mix in chili powder and sugar. Taste. Add more chili powder if desired, and salt and pepper if needed.

4. Place tongue slices in sauce and simmer 20 to 30 minutes.

5. Serve on a hot platter with some of the sauce over the slices. Arrange potatoes round them.

The tongue can be cooked at any time, then sliced and simmered in the sauce just before serving.

Suggested Menu: ONION SOUP; FRESH BEEF TONGUE CREOLE; PARSLEY POTATOES; CHOPPED BUTTERED SPINACH; carrot and raisin salad, FRENCH DRESSING; TINNED PEACHES IN WINE.

VEAL CHOPS AU BEURRE, TOMATO-EGG SAUCE

SERVES 4 · 35 MINUTES

4 *veal chops, pounded thin*	$\frac{1}{4}$ *teaspoon salt*
2 *tablespoons butter*	$\frac{1}{8}$ *teaspoon white pepper*

TOMATO-EGG SAUCE

1 *teaspoon tomato paste*	1 *teaspoon vinegar or lemon*
3 *tablespoons cream*	*juice*
1 *raw egg yolk*	$\frac{1}{4}$ *teaspoon salt*
$\frac{1}{4}$ *teaspoon water*	*Pinch white pepper*
	1 *tablespoon butter*

1. Wipe chops with a damp paper towel.

2. Melt butter in a pan over moderate heat. Sauté chops until brown. Season with salt and pepper. Brown other side. If not

31

cooked through, reduce heat, cover, and cook until tender. Remove to a hot serving dish.

3. To make TOMATO-EGG SAUCE, blend tomato paste with cream. Mix egg yolk with water, vinegar, salt, and pepper, Scrape pan to loosen browned particles. Place pan over low heat. Add butter and when it melts, stir in cream-tomato mixture. Blend for a few seconds and remove from heat. Slowly stir in egg mixture. Now hold pan an inch above low heat and keep stirring to warm up sauce. This sauce will curdle if it gets hot.

4. Cover each chop with a spoonful of sauce and serve.

Suggested Menu: SUMMER VEGETABLE RELISH BOWL; VEAL CHOPS AU BEURRE, TOMATO-EGG SAUCE; ASPARAGUS WITH BUTTERED CRUMBS; puréed potatoes; ITALIAN TOMATO SALAD; PEACH MELBA.

✄ VEAL CHOPS IN WHITE WINE

SERVES 3 TO 6 · $1\frac{1}{4}$ TO $1\frac{3}{4}$ HOURS

6 *loin veal chops*	$\frac{1}{2}$ *teaspoon salt*
1 *clove garlic*	$\frac{1}{4}$ *teaspoon pepper*
1 *tablespoon minced parsley*	1 *bay leaf*
1 *tablespoon oil*	$\frac{1}{2}$ *cup dry white wine*
1 *tablespoon butter*	$\frac{1}{4}$ *cup chicken stock*

1. Wipe veal with a damp paper towel. Split garlic clove and mince parsley. Heat oil and butter in a skillet over medium-low heat. Cook garlic until light brown. Discard it. Add chops and brown quickly. Add salt, pepper, bay leaf, and parsley. Cook 1 minute, stirring to blend seasoning.

2. Add wine. Cover and simmer until about 2 or 3 tablespoons of wine are left. Baste every 15 minutes. This should take about 1 to $1\frac{1}{2}$ hours. Add more wine if more liquid is needed during this time.

3. Stir in stock and simmer chops 15 minutes or until tender.

When ready, the chops should be covered with a delicious glaze.

Suggested Menu: MOULES MARINIÈRE; VEAL CHOPS IN WHITE WINE; POTATOES MAÎTRE D'HÔTEL; braised celery; salad of cubed beets, MUSTARD CREAM DRESSING (see CELERY SALAD); RASPBERRY-PEACH SHERBET.

⅄ BLANQUETTE DE VEAU

SERVES 4 · 1½ TO 1¾ HOURS

2 *pounds veal from leg or rump, cubed*	¼ *teaspoon salt*
	⅛ *teaspoon white pepper*
2 *cups cold chicken stock*	*Pinch thyme*
1 *carrot*	2 *peppercorns*
1 *rib celery*	2 *tablespoons butter*
1 *leek, white part only*	2 *tablespoons flour*
(optional)	1 *egg yolk*
1 *small white turnip*	1 *tablespoon cream or milk*
(optional)	*Salt to taste*
2 *sprigs parsley*	*Dash cayenne*
1 *onion stuck with 1 clove*	½ *teaspoon lemon juice*
1 *small bay leaf*	*Paprika*

1. Put veal and stock in a saucepan, bring to a boil, and skim. Slice carrot, celery, leek, and turnip. Add these to saucepan with parsley, onion, bay leaf, salt, pepper, thyme, and peppercorns. Cook slowly about 1¼ to 1½ hours until tender.

2. Remove veal from broth and keep it warm. Strain broth.

3. Melt butter in a pan. Away from heat, blend in flour until smooth. Return to heat and add 1 cup broth gradually, stirring constantly until sauce comes to a boil. Reduce heat and simmer. Beat egg yolk slightly in a small bowl. Mix in

33

cream or milk and then slowly 3 tablespoons of the hot sauce. Stir mixture gradually into remainder of sauce. Add salt and cayenne. Mix in lemon juice. Do not allow sauce to boil.

4. Arrange meat in the centre of a hot platter. Spoon some sauce over it and pass additional sauce in gravy dish. Arrange RICE PILAF or BOILED RICE around veal with a sprinkling of paprika.

Suggested Menu: FLEMISH SALAD; BLANQUETTE DE VEAU; RICE PILAF or BOILED RICE; sautéed whole mushrooms; sugared sliced strawberries in melon rings.

✂ CASSEROLE OF VEAL WITH SOUR CREAM
SERVES 6 · 1¾ HOURS

3 *pounds veal from leg or rump, cubed*	¾ *cup liquid made up of tinned mushroom liquor and water*
1 *small onion*	
1 *small tin (4 ounces) sliced mushrooms*	1 *tinned pimento*
	1 *tablespoon chopped parsley*
1½ *tablespoons butter*	
½ *teaspoon salt*	1 *teaspoon Worcester Sauce*
⅛ *teaspoon pepper*	1 *teaspoon butter*
2 *tablespoons flour*	½ *cup sour cream*
¾ *cup dry white wine*	

1. Wipe veal with a damp paper towel. Mince onion. Drain mushrooms. Reserve liquor.

2. Melt butter in a frying-pan over low heat. Sauté meat until light brown. Season with salt and pepper. Turn and brown other side. Toss in onions and let them colour slightly 1 minute. Sprinkle flour over meat and onions. Stir to blend. Add wine and other liquid. Bring to a boil.

3. Mince pimento. Chop parsley. Add with Worcester Sauce to pan and stir. Transfer contents of pan to a casserole or other saucepan. Simmer covered 1¼ hours.

4. Cook mushrooms in hot butter 2 minutes. Add to meat. Remove casserole from heat. Blend in sour cream, a little at a time, with saucepan liquor. Return to low heat to warm up sauce. Do not allow it to boil. Add more salt or pepper if necessary.

5. Serve in the casserole or transfer to a deep platter.

Suggested Menu: CRAB MEAT SALAD; CASSEROLE OF VEAL WITH SOUR CREAM; buttered noodles; BROCCOLI SALAD; FROZEN ZABAIONE.

ROLLED VEAL

SERVES 4 · 45 MINUTES

1 *pound veal slices, 4 by 5 inches, and ¼-inch thick*	2 *celery ribs*
¼ *teaspoon salt in all*	4 *tablespoons cooked ham*
¼ *teaspoon pepper in all*	2 *tablespoons butter*
½ *small packet cream cheese*	¼ *cup plus 2 tablespoons port*
	1 *teaspoon chopped parsley*

1. Have several toothpicks or some light string handy.

2. Pound veal slices to required thinness. Trim ragged edges. Season each slice with salt and pepper.

3. In a small bowl, soften cheese with a fork. Mince celery and ham. Add to cheese and blend.

4. Distribute mixture on veal slices. Roll up and fasten with toothpicks or string. If using string, tie each end of roll.

5. Melt butter slowly in a skillet. Add rolls and cook until they are well browned all over.

6. Stir in ¼ cup wine. Cover and cook slowly 20 to 25 minutes. Prepare parsley for garnish. Baste veal with sauce occasionally. Turn once. When wine has almost cooked away, add the remaining 2 tablespoons and swish round for 1 minute. Serve rolls sprinkled with chopped parsley.

Suggested Menu: MINESTRONE; ROLLED VEAL; SPANISH RICE; CREAMED SPINACH; salad of lettuce, sliced red radish, and black olives, FRENCH DRESSING; fresh fruit cup, assorted cheeses (see CHEESE AND FRUIT FOR DESSERT).

⚡ CALVES LIVER, AUSTRIAN STYLE

SERVES 4 · 20 MINUTES

1 *pound fresh calves liver*	1 *tablespoon chopped chives*
¼ *cup flour*	*or parsley*
½ *teaspoon salt*	3 *tablespoons butter*
⅛ *teaspoon pepper*	¼ *cup dry white wine*
½ *teaspoon paprika*	½ *cup sour cream*

1. Remove tubes and outer skin from liver. Cut liver into narrow strips. Have a hot platter ready.

2. Combine flour, salt, pepper, and paprika. Coat strips with mixture. Chop chives or parsley.

3. Melt butter in a skillet. When it is hot, brown liver quickly on both sides over medium heat, tossing 3 or 4 minutes to brown. Remove to platter.

4. Add wine to skillet; scrape pan to blend in liver particles. Mix in sour cream, a little at a time to prevent curdling. Warm sauce over low heat, but do not allow it to boil. Taste for additional seasoning. Return liver to pan; mix with sauce.

5. Serve at once with sprinkling of chopped herb.

Try this with buttered noodles prepared with or without tiny croûtons.

Suggested Menu: MEAT SALAD VINAIGRETTE; CALVES LIVER, AUSTRIAN STYLE; CARROTS VICHY; RICE PILAF WITH GREEN PEAS, LADYFINGER PUDDING, APRICOT-ORANGE SAUCE.

LAMB STEW PRINTANIER

SERVES 4 · 2¾ TO 3 HOURS

2½ pounds lamb, breast, neck, or shoulder, cubed
1 tablespoon oil
½ teaspoon salt
¼ teaspoon pepper
Good pinch sugar
1 tablespoon flour
1 cup hot water
1 chicken bouillon cube
2 tablespoons tomato paste
1 clove garlic, crushed
4 sprigs parsley
1 bay leaf
⅛ teaspoon powdered thyme
8 small white onions
8 small new potatoes
4 young whole carrots
2 small white turnips
1 tablespoon butter
1 piece lemon peel, an inch square (white part removed)
¼ cup hot water
1 pound green beans, cut in half

1. Trim fat from lamb.
2. Heat oil in a saucepan and brown lamb cubes over brisk heat. Season as they brown with salt, pepper, and sugar. This should take about 5 to 6 minutes. Sprinkle with flour and turn to blend with fat. Add cup of hot water and stir until it comes to a boil. Add chicken cube, tomato paste, crushed garlic, parsley, bay leaf, and thyme. Cover and simmer 1½ hours.
3. Peel onions, potatoes, and carrots, and cube turnips. Toss them in hot butter over low heat 3 to 4 minutes.
4. Remove lamb to casserole or saucepan. Add vegetables. Skim fat from broth. Strain broth over meat and vegetables. Mince lemon peel and add with ¼ cup of hot water. Bring to a boil. Cook slowly 1 hour, basting occasionally. Add salt if needed.
5. Twenty minutes before meat is done, cook beans separately in very little boiling salted water. Uncover after 5 minutes to help preserve green colour. Cook 15 to 20 minutes more until beans are tender but crisp. There should be just 2 to 3 tablespoons of

liquid left. Add it to broth if broth has cooked down considerably.

6. Mix beans with stew and serve from casserole or in serving bowl.

Should you wish to eliminate the white onions, be sure to cook 1 medium-sized yellow one, sliced or chopped, with the stew. The lemon peel imparts a delightful fragrance to the stew.

Suggested Menu: CURRIED LOBSTER ON TOAST; LAMB STEW PRINTANIER; spring vegetables cooked with stew; salad of tomato and water cress, FRENCH DRESSING; sliced sugared strawberries in liqueur (see SERVING FRUIT WITH LIQUEUR).

⅍ LAMB AND RICE PILAF

SERVES 4 TO 6 · 2 TO 2¼ HOURS

2 *pounds lamb cutlets cut*
   from leg, cubed
1 *medium-sized onion*
1 *tablespoon butter*
1 *tablespoon oil*
½ *teaspoon salt*
⅛ *teaspoon pepper*
¾ *cup hot chicken or light*
   beef stock

1 *tablespoon oil*
1 *cup raw rice*
1½ *cups hot chicken or beef*
   stock
1 *small bay leaf*
3 *peppercorns*

1. Remove fat from meat. Mince onion.

2. Place butter and oil in a large heavy saucepan over medium-low heat. When it is hot, brown lamb cubes quickly on all sides, adding onion when the browning process is three-quarters finished. Season with salt and pepper.

3. Add ¾ cups hot stock and bring to boil. Simmer covered until meat is tender, about 1½ hours. Correct seasoning.

38

4. A few minutes before meat is done, heat oil in a small frying-pan. Sauté rice slowly 6 to 7 minutes, turning occasionally with spatula to let rice colour evenly. Add it to lamb. Cover with 1½ cups stock, add bay leaf and peppercorns. Bring to boil. Reduce heat, cover, and simmer 18 to 20 minutes. The liquid should be mostly absorbed and rice tender. If there is not enough liquid to cook rice, add a little more hot stock. Remove bay leaf and peppercorns if possible.

5. To serve, fluff up rice with 2 forks. Turn pilaf out into a deep serving dish or on to a platter. Serve piping hot.

Suggested Menu: curried cream cheese on saltines, with pine-apple juice (if you're not having a cocktail); LAMB AND RICE PILAF; AUBERGINE CREOLE; lettuce salad, FRENCH DRESSING; AVOCADO IN KIRSCH.

LAMB CASSEROLE WITH WINE

SERVES 4 · 2¾ HOURS

2 to 2½ pounds lamb shoulder, breast, or neck	Salt to taste
	⅛ teaspoon pepper
1 tablespoon butter	4 medium-sized carrots
2 tablespoons brandy	2 small turnips
1½ tablespoons flour	8 small white onions
1 cup hot water	2 tablespoons butter
½ cup dry red wine or ¼ cup sherry	½ pound mushrooms
	1 pound green peas
1 teaspoon tomato paste	2 tablespoons chopped chives or parsley
1 chicken bouillon cube	

1. Melt butter in a casserole over medium-low heat. When it is hot, brown lamb on all sides. Add brandy. Touch a lighted match to it and when flame begins to die down, cover casserole for a moment to seal in the aroma.

2. Stir in flour. Add water, red wine or sherry, and tomato paste; bring to boil. Add bouillon cube, crush, and mix. Season with a little salt and the pepper. Cook slowly 1½ hours.

3. Skim fat from broth. Slice carrots and turnips, peel onions, and brown all lightly in butter. Add to lamb. Add more stock if needed to cook vegetables. Cook slowly covered 20 minutes. Halve mushrooms, shell peas, and add. Cook· 20 more minutes or until meat and vegetables are tender.

4. Remove to a serving dish and sprinkle with chopped chives or parsley.

Try to get fresh chives for garnish if possible; they give a surprising lift to lamb.

Suggested Menu: chilled tomato juice; LAMB CASSEROLE WITH WINE; vegetables from casserole; CHIVE POTATOES; mixed green salad (see TOSSED SALAD), FRENCH DRESSING; LADY-FINGER PUDDING, SHERRY SAUCE.

✻ LAMB AND AUBERGINE STEW

SERVES 4 · 2 TO 2¼ HOURS

2 to 2½ *pounds lamb for stewing*	1 *small tin tomato paste:* 6 *ounces*
1 *medium-sized onion*	1 *cup hot water*
1 *clove garlic*	¼ *teaspoon powdered thyme*
1 *small aubergine*	⅛ *teaspoon pepper*
2 *tablespoons oil*	2 *tablespoons chopped chives*
½ *teaspoon salt*	*or parsley*

1. Mince onion and garlic. Cut unpeeled aubergine into large cubes.

2. Heat oil in a skillet over moderate-low heat. Add onion, garlic, and aubergine; season with ¼ teaspoon of salt and brown

40

lightly. Remove to a saucepan. Add more fat if needed and sear lamb quickly. Add to vegetables with tomato paste, water, thyme, ¼ teaspoon of salt, and pepper. Simmer covered until meat is tender, about 1¾ to 2 hours. Aubergine should be dissolved in sauce. Skim off fat. Chop chives or parsley.

3. Serve stew over rice. Sprinkle lamb with chives or parsley.

Suggested Menu: chilled melon slices; LAMB AND AUBERGINE STEW; RICE PILAF WITH RAISINS AND PINE NUTS; salad of chilled peas, tomato, and shredded lettuce, with chopped fresh mint or tarragon; MERINGUE PUFFS ON LEMON-WINE CUSTARD.

⅄ LAMB AND LIMA BEAN CASSEROLE

SERVES 4 · 2½ HOURS

2 *pounds shoulder of lamb, cubed*	½ *teaspoon monosodium glutamate (Accent)*
¾ *cup soaked lima beans*	2 *tablespoons chopped parsley*
1 *small onion*	4 *small whole carrots*
1 *clove garlic*	2 *ribs celery with leaves*
1 *tablespoon oil*	½ *teaspoon oregano,*
½ *teaspoon salt*	*powdered in fingers*
¼ *teaspoon pepper*	3 *tablespoons sherry*
3 *cups hot chicken broth*	*(optional)*
¼ *cup tomato juice*	

1. Have ready lima beans which have soaked in cold water overnight.

2. Trim fat from lamb. Mince onion and garlic.

3. Heat oil in a skillet over moderate heat and brown lamb quickly. Season with salt and pepper as it browns. Remove meat to a casserole. Sauté onion and garlic slowly 3 or 4 minutes. Pour off any fat. Add broth and scrape skillet to loosen particles. Pour into casserole.

4. Add tomato juice, Accent, and drained beans. Bring to a boil. Simmer covered 1 hour. Correct seasoning.

5. Prepare parsley, carrots, and celery. Add these to casserole and cook 30 minutes. Add oregano and sherry and cook 30 minutes more. Remove celery.

6. Remove lamb to a hot platter. Spoon beans and carrots around it.

Suggested Menu: ANCHOVY AND TOMATO SALAD; LAMB AND LIMA BEAN CASSEROLE; lima beans and carrots from casserole; SPINACH SALAD, SPICY DRESSING; COCONUT PUDDING, JIFFY RUM SAUCE.

⅍ PORK CHOPS IN WHITE WINE

SERVES 3 TO 6 · 1½ TO 1¾ HOURS

6 *pork chops, centre cut*	2 *tablespoons butter*
1 *large onion*	¾ *cup dry white wine*
¾ *teaspoon dry mustard*	*A little chicken broth or water*
1½ *teaspoons salt*	*if necessary*
½ *teaspoon pepper*	

1. Remove most of fat from chops. Slice onion thinly.

2. Blend mustard, salt, and pepper. Rub into both sides of chops.

3. Melt butter (or bits of pork fat) in a large skillet over moderate heat. Brown chops well on both sides. Remove them from pan. Add onion and cook 3 minutes.

4. Stir in wine and return chops to skillet. Cover and simmer until chops are tender, about 1¼ hours. If more liquid is needed, add a few tablespoons of broth or water. Chops should be well glazed when done. Serve on a hot platter.

Suggested Menu: AVOCADO-LIVER PÂTÉ on crackers, tomato juice; PORK CHOPS IN WHITE WINE; buttered noodles with caraway seeds; buttered sliced beets; mixed green salad (see TOSSED SALAD), FRENCH DRESSING made with lemon juice; RUM-GLAZED APPLES.

⚶ PORK CHOPS IN RED WINE

SERVES 3 TO 6 · $1\frac{1}{2}$ TO $1\frac{3}{4}$ HOURS

6 *pork chops, centre cut*	$\frac{1}{2}$ *cup red wine*
2 *cloves garlic*	$\frac{1}{4}$ *teaspoon salt*
Good handful parsley	$\frac{1}{8}$ *teaspoon black pepper*

1. Trim fat from chops. Cut some of it into small dice and melt in a skillet. Brown chops quickly over medium heat on both sides.

2. Mince garlic. Mince parsley, reserving 1 tablespoon for later use. Add garlic and parsley to pork and sauté 3 minutes.

3. Add wine, salt, pepper. Cover and simmer $1\frac{1}{4}$ hours or until tender. Baste occasionally. Add additional wine if too much evaporates. When chops are done, there should be just a few tablespoons of liquid left, and the chops should be glazed.

4. Sprinkle some pan sauce over each chop before serving. Dust with remaining parsley.

Suggested Menu: CARROTS À LA GRECQUE; PORK CHOPS IN RED WINE; mashed sweet potatoes; STEAMED CHOPPED BROCCOLI; BRANDIED APPLE SAUCE WITH RAISINS.

❧ BARBECUED PORK CHOPS

SERVES 3 TO 6 · 1¾ HOURS

6 *large pork chops*	1 *large onion*
¼ *teaspoon salt*	1 *green pepper*

BARBECUE SAUCE

1 *small bottle tomato sauce*	2 *tablespoons lemon juice*
6 ounces	1 *teaspoon chili powder*
1 *cup water*	½ *teaspoon salt*
1 *tablespoon Worcester*	½ *teaspoon prepared*
Sauce	*mustard*
1 *tablespoon brown sugar*	

3 *to 6 small sweet or white*
potatoes

1. Wipe chops with a damp paper towel. Cut off most of fat. Melt bits of fat in a frying-pan. Brown chops on both sides. Season with salt as they brown.

2. Mince onion and green pepper. Remove chops from pan. Add vegetables. Sauté them 2 minutes. Drain off excess fat. Return chops to pan.

3. In a saucepan combine 8 ingredients listed under Barbecue Sauce. Bring to a boil.

4. Pour half of sauce over chops. Cover and simmer 1 hour.

5. Parboil potatoes. Drain. Place them over chops. Add enough sauce to half cover potatoes. Raise heat a little and cook 20 to 25 minutes or until tender. Serve chops surrounded by potatoes, with sauce spooned over meat.

Suggested Menu: SHERRIED CHEESE PÂTÉ on toast fingers or crackers; BARBECUED PORK CHOPS; potatoes cooked with chops; chilled cut green bean salad with small pickled onions, FRENCH DRESSING; BRANDIED APPLE FRITTERS.

❧ HAM IN SHERRY SAUCE

SERVES 4 · 40 TO 50 MINUTES EXCLUSIVE OF SOAKING

2 *slices pre-cooked tenderized*	1 *tablespoon sherry*
ham, 1 inch thick	2 *tablespoons butter*
2 *tablespoons brown sugar*	$\frac{1}{4}$ *to* $\frac{1}{2}$ *cup milk*
1 *teaspoon prepared mustard*	

1. Soak ham in milk to cover for 1 hour if it is salty. Drain and dry it well. Cut off most of fat.
2. Blend sugar, mustard, and sherry. Brush half of mixture on one side of ham.
3. Melt butter in a skillet over moderate heat. Place ham, brushed side down, in pan and sear quickly until browned. Spread remaining mixture on ham. Turn and sear.
4. Add milk and stir to mix with sugar and juices in pan. Cover and simmer 30 to 40 minutes. Baste occasionally with liquid in pan. Serve on a hot platter, with remaining sauce spooned over it.

A really good ham dish. Be especially careful to make no substitutions of ingredients if flavour is to be retained.

Suggested Menu: GUACAMOLE on tomato slices; HAM IN SHERRY SAUCE; CREAMED SPINACH; KIDNEY BEAN SALAD; PARADISE PUDDING, APPLE-CRANBERRY SAUCE.

❧ STOVE-TOP ROAST CHICKEN

SERVES 4 · $1\frac{1}{2}$ HOURS

A $3\frac{1}{2}$-*pound fryer, left whole*	1 *tablespoon butter*
$\frac{1}{2}$ *lemon*	$\frac{1}{2}$ *teaspoon salt*
$\frac{1}{2}$ *teaspoon salt*	$\frac{1}{4}$ *teaspoon pepper*
$\frac{1}{8}$ *teaspoon pepper*	2 *tablespoons chopped onion*
8 *cloves garlic*	$\frac{1}{4}$ *cup brandy or cognac*
8 *sprigs parsley*	$\frac{1}{4}$ *cup dry white wine*
2 *tablespoons oil*	*Good pinch thyme*

45

1. Rub cleaned, dried chicken with lemon, inside and out, squeezing juice. Rub salt and pepper into cavity.
2. Peel garlic and split it into halves. Chop parsley coarsely. Stuff one cut garlic clove and a little parsley into neck cavity. Sew up opening with needle and thread. Stuff remaining garlic and parsley into body cavity. Sew up opening. Tie legs and tail together with string. Fold wings at joint and tie close to body.
3. Heat oil and butter in a heavy skillet just a little larger than the chicken. Brown chicken all over. Start with medium-high heat, lower to medium, and then to low. Season chicken as it browns. Browning takes about 10 to 15 minutes.
4. Place browned chicken in a casserole. Top with onion. Pour brandy carefully over it. Touch a lighted match to chicken and let brandy blaze up for a few seconds. When flame is about to die down, cover casserole for a moment. Remove cover and add wine and thyme. Cover and simmer for 30 minutes. Turn bird over and simmer 30 minutes. Baste every 15 minutes. If liquid cooks out, add a tablespoon or more of water.
5. Transfer chicken to a warm platter. Remove strings and threads. Discard stuffing. Cut chicken into serving pieces. Serve with a little pan juice.

Don't be alarmed by the quantity of garlic. It flavours the chicken delicately.

Suggested Menu: FISH IN VINEGAR-RAISIN SAUCE; STOVE-TOP ROAST CHICKEN; RICE PIEMONTAISE; ASPARAGUS FLAMANDE; tomatoes stuffed with CELERY SALAD; MÉLANGE OF RASP-BERRIES AND PEACHES.

✄ COQ AU VIN · Rooster Braised in Wine
SERVES 4 · 1½ TO 1¾ HOURS

1 *fryer, cut into serving portions*	¼ *cup flour*
	1 *teaspoon salt*

¼ *teaspoon pepper*	1 *cup raw ham*
1 *tablespoon oil*	¼ *cup brandy*
1 *tablespoon butter*	1 *cup dry white or red wine*
8 *to* 10 *small white onions*	1 *bay leaf*
1 *clove garlic*	¼ *teaspoon thyme*
1 *tablespoon chopped parsley*	¼ *pound mushrooms*

1. Combine flour, salt, and pepper. Coat chicken with mixture.
2. Heat oil and butter over moderate heat in an oval casserole or heavy saucepan. Brown chicken on both sides.
3. While chicken browns, peel onions, mince garlic, chop parsley, and cube ham.
4. Add onions and garlic to chicken and turn in fat 1 minute. Pour brandy over chicken. Light it with match. When flame begins to die down, cover pan for a moment to preserve aroma.
5. Add wine, parsley, ham, bay leaf, and thyme. Cover and simmer about 1 hour. Slice mushrooms; add and stir. Simmer 15 minutes or until chicken is tender.

Suggested Menu: SHRIMP VINAIGRETTE; COQ AU VIN; PARSLEY POTATOES; buttered carrots; endive salad; ENGLISH SALAD DRESSING; CHERRIES JUBILEE.

⅍ PORTUGUESE CHICKEN SAUTÉ

SERVES 2 TO 3 · 1¼ HOURS

1 *broiler, quartered*	1 *clove garlic*
1 *teaspoon salt*	1 *small onion*
¼ *teaspoon pepper*	½ *cup sliced mushrooms*
2 *tablespoons olive oil*	1 *teaspoon chopped parsley*
1 *tablespoon butter*	1 *tablespoon dry white wine*
2 *large tomatoes*	

47

1. Rub salt and pepper into chicken. Heat oil and butter in a frying-pan or casserole. Cook chicken about 15 minutes over medium-low heat until it is brown all over. Remove it from pan.

2. While chicken browns, peel and chop tomatoes, discarding seeds but saving juice. Mince garlic and chop onion.

3. Leave only enough fat in pan to sauté onion and garlic. Cook 3 minutes. Add tomatoes with their juice, sliced mushrooms, chopped parsley, and wine. Stir. Cover and simmer 45 minutes. Correct seasoning. Simmer 10 more minutes or until tender.

4. Arrange chicken parts on a hot platter or serve in casserole.

Suggested Menu: VICHYSSOISE; PORTUGUESE CHICKEN SAUTÉ; salad of chilled, cooked mixed frozen vegetables, MUSTARD CREAM DRESSING (SEE CELERY SALAD); FRUIT COMPÔTE.

CHICKEN MARENGO

SERVES 4 · 1½ TO 1¾ HOURS

1 *frying chicken, cut up*	1 *tablespoon flour*
½ *pound mushrooms*	1 *tablespoon tomato paste*
2 *tablespoons butter*	6 *tablespoons dry white wine*
2 *tablespoons olive oil*	6 *tablespoons water*
¼ *teaspoon salt*	1 *chicken bouillon cube*
⅛ *teaspoon pepper*	1 *clove garlic, crushed*
2 *medium-sized tomatoes*	1 *tablespoon chopped parsley*

1. Slice mushrooms. Melt butter in a large saucepan over moderate heat. Turn mushrooms round in hot butter 2 minutes. Remove from pan.

2. Add oil and heat. Brown chicken pieces well. Season with salt and pepper. While chicken browns, peel, seed, and chop tomatoes. Save juice. When chicken is brown, sprinkle pieces with flour and stir.

3. Add tomatoes and juice, tomato paste, wine, water, bouillon cube, crushed garlic, and mushrooms. Bring to boil. Stir to dissolve cube. Cover and simmer 1 to 1¼ hours or until tender. Baste occasionally with pan liquid. The last half hour remove cover so that sauce can reduce somewhat. Correct seasoning.

4. Chop parsley. Place chicken on a hot serving dish. Cover with sauce and dust with parsley.

Olive oil is a must in this dish to give it its characteristic flavour. The original dish is reputed to have been created by one of Napoleon's chefs who, during a military campaign at Marengo, ran out of butter and used olive oil to cook his chicken.

Suggested Menu: CHICKEN LIVER PÂTÉ on soda biscuits; CHICKEN MARENGO; RICE PILAF; buttered green peas; salad of chicory and small black olives, FRENCH DRESSING; Danish Blue cheese and pears, or Cheddar cheese and apples, with crackers (see CHEESE AND FRUIT FOR DESSERT).

❥ CHICKEN PAPRIKA

SERVES 4 · 2¾ HOURS MINIMUM

A 3½-pound fryer, cut into parts
Soup greens
1½ cups water
1 chicken bouillon cube
1 cup sour cream
½ cup flour
2 teaspoons paprika
1 teaspoon salt
¼ teaspoon pepper
¼ teaspoon powdered ginger
2 or 3 dashes cayenne
1 tablespoon oil

1 tablespoon butter
1 tablespoon Worcester Sauce
1 tablespoon chili sauce
1 large clove garlic, crushed
¼ teaspoon salt
3 tablespoons sherry
1 small tin sliced mushrooms
1 teaspoon potato flour or potato starch
1 tinned pimento, cut into strips

1. (This may be done the day before the chicken is to be served.) Remove skin from chicken. Remove the larger bones. Leave chicken in large pieces. Simmer skin, bones, wings, giblets, and soup greens with water and bouillon cube for 45 minutes. Strain, chill, and remove fat from broth. (Or substitute 1 cup of tinned chicken broth.) Blend 1 cup cold broth with sour cream and let stand at least 1 hour or overnight.

2. In a paper bag, combine flour, paprika, salt, pepper, ginger, and cayenne. Shake chicken in mixture to coat. Heat oil and butter in a skillet over medium heat. When mixture is hot, brown chicken pieces quickly all over.

3. In a casserole or oval shallow saucepan, combine broth-cream mixture with Worcester Sauce, chili sauce, crushed garlic, salt, and sherry. Heat to boiling point. Add chicken. The pieces should be no more than $\frac{3}{4}$ submerged in the sauce. If there is too much sauce, save some to add later when it has cooked down. Cover and simmer until chicken is almost tender, about $1\frac{1}{4}$ hours. Drain mushrooms. Add them.

4. Remove 2 tablespoonsful of sauce and cool it. Blend with potato flour away from flame. Add to sauce in pan and mix. Let it come to a boil once, stirring constantly. Reduce heat and simmer 10 minutes.

5. Add pimento and cook 1 minute.

6. Serve from casserole or on a hot platter with some of the sauce spooned over chicken. Serve extra sauce in sauceboat.

A fine dish for entertaining. You may wish to add a few cooked green peas for texture and colour.

Suggested Menu: celery stuffed with cream cheese-caviar spread (see CREAM CHEESE-RED CAVIAR CANAPES); CHICKEN PAPRIKA; buttered noodles; GREEN BEANS AMANDINE; salad of sliced red radish, scallion, cucumber, tomato, lettuce, FRENCH DRESSING; TUTTI-FRUTTI FROZEN PUDDING.

☇ CHICKEN CACCIATORE

SERVES 4 · 1½ TO 1¾ HOURS

A 3-pound chicken, cut up	*1 green pepper*
¼ cup flour	*1 teaspoon chopped parsley*
1¼ teaspoons salt	*1 clove garlic*
¼ teaspoon pepper	*1 teaspoon salt*
¼ cup olive oil	*⅛ teaspoon pepper*
1 tin tomatoes: 3½ cups	*1 teaspoon oregano*

1. Blend flour, salt, and pepper in a paper bag. Shake chicken parts in mixture and coat lightly.
2. Heat oil in a large skillet over moderate heat. Brown chicken until it is golden on both sides.
3. While chicken browns, strain tomatoes, mince green pepper, chop parsley, and crush garlic.
4. Pour off excess fat. Add tomatoes, green pepper, salt, pepper, oregano, parsley, and garlic. Bring to a boil and stir. Cover and cook slowly 1 to 1½ hours, until chicken is tender.

A bottle of Chianti turns this robust dinner into a feast.

Suggested Menu: ANCHOVY AND PIMENTO SALAD; CHICKEN CACCIATORE; buttered spaghetti with Parmesan cheese; CHOPPED SPINACH; lemon sherbet with rum.

✄ CHICKEN COTLETKI · Patties

SERVES 4 · 45 MINUTES

2 *cups uncooked meat from*	*Pinch nutmeg*
chicken breasts, ground finely	1 *egg yolk*
1 *slice crustless white bread*	1 *tablespoon sweet or sour*
Milk for soaking bread	*cream*
1 *small onion*	1 *tablespoon melted butter*
1 *tablespoon parsley*	¼ *cup flour*
½ *teaspoon salt*	3 *tablespoons butter*
¼ *teaspoon pepper*	½ *cup sour cream*

1. Soak bread in a little milk. Squeeze dry. Fluff up. Put chicken through grinder twice. Chop onion and parsley finely; combine them with chicken, bread, seasonings, egg yolk, cream, and butter. Mixture should be well seasoned.

2. Shape into balls. Dip them into flour and flatten them into patties. Melt butter. When it is hot, sauté patties over moderate heat until they are golden brown on both sides.

3. Remove them from pan and keep them warm. Mix sour cream with butter in pan and heat through. Pour sauce over patties.

Suggested Menu: COLD SALMON, MAYONNAISE CAPER SAUCE; CHICKEN COTLETKI; puréed potatoes; buttered peas; beet, cucumber, and onion salad, FRENCH DRESSING; vanilla ice cream, RASPBERRY SAUCE.

✄ QUICK CHICKEN CURRY

SERVES 4 · 45 MINUTES

2 *to 3 cups cooked chicken*	1 *to 2 tablespoons curry*
1 *large onion*	*powder to taste*
1 *green pepper*	2 *cups hot chicken broth*
1 *apple with peel*	1 *tablespoon cornflour*
2 *tablespoons butter*	¼ *cup cold chicken broth*

52

1. Dice onion; chop green pepper and apple finely.

2. Melt butter in a pan and cook onion slowly 2 minutes. Add green pepper and apple; cook until they are tender.

3. Blend in curry powder and cook 1 minute. Add broth and bring to a boil. Cover and simmer 30 minutes.

4. While sauce simmers, cube chicken. Blend cornflour into cold broth. Stir it into curry sauce. Boil gently 2 minutes. Add chicken, and heat slowly.

5. Serve curry hot over a bed of boiled rice.

Suggested Menu: EGG DROP SOUP; QUICK CHICKEN CURRY; BOILED RICE; VICHY CARROTS; PINEAPPLE-COTTAGE CHEESE SALAD; jellied cranberry sauce; FRENCH FRITTERS with powdered sugar.

❧ CHICKEN ENCHILADAS, MEXICAN CHILI SAUCE

SERVES 4 TO 6 · 1¼ HOURS

2 *cups* MEXICAN CHILI SAUCE
14 *pancakes*
1 *tablespoon brandy*
  (optional)
½ *cup blanched almonds*
3 *to* 3½ *cups cooked chicken*
¼ *cup heart of celery*
¼ *cup Bermuda onion*
  (optional)
1 *tablespoon chopped parsley*
Salt and pepper
2 *to* 3 *tablespoons butter*

1. Prepare MEXICAN CHILI SAUCE.

2. Make pancakes (see CHEESE BLINTZES) but omit sugar and add 1 tablespoon brandy (optional).

3. Coarsely chop and toast almonds. Mince chicken. Chop celery, onion, and parsley. Mix all with ½ cup MEXICAN CHILI SAUCE and season to taste with salt and pepper if needed.

4. Place about 2 heaped tablespoons of filling on each pancake. Fold into envelope shape. Sauté, seamside down, in hot butter.

When pancakes are crisp and brown, turn with spatula and crisp other side.

5. Serve enchiladas hot with rice. Pass remaining sauce.

⅄ MEXICAN CHILI SAUCE

MAKES 2 CUPS · 20 MINUTES

8 *ounces tinned Italian tomatoes*	2½ *tablespoons flour*
1 *small onion*	1 *tablespoon chili powder*
1 *small green pepper*	¾ *cup water*
2 *tablespoons butter*	1 *chicken bouillon cube*
	Salt to taste

1. Strain tomatoes to remove seeds. Set aside.
2. Chop onion and pepper. Sauté them in hot butter over low heat until soft.
3. Combine flour and chili powder. Sprinkle these over vegetables, stirring a few seconds to blend.
4. Add water, bouillon cube, and tomatoes. Stir constantly until sauce boils and thickens. Be sure cube is dissolved. Add salt if needed. Simmer 10 minutes.
5. Serve sauce hot.

This is not a hot, hot sauce. It is good with rice, dried beans, meat balls, and in making stews from leftovers. It will keep several days.

Suggested Menu: chicken broth; CHICKEN ENCHILADAS, MEXICAN CHILI SAUCE; RICE PILAF; GUACAMOLE; sliced melon (or mango, if you can get it).

A complicated menu, but fortunately much can be prepared ahead. Cook and mince chicken and prepare sauce a day in advance. Refrigerate. In the morning or afternoon before dinner, make and fill pancakes. Keep all under refrigeration. Just before dinner, prepare rice, make salad, and crisp pancakes. Heat broth and sauce.

⅍ BRAISED DUCK À L'ORANGE

SERVES 3 · 2½ HOURS

*A 4- to 4½-pound duck, cut
  into serving pieces
1 small carrot
1 small onion
2 mushrooms
1 clove garlic
Peel of 1 orange
2 tablespoons butter
2 sprigs parsley
1 teaspoon salt*

*⅛ teaspoon pepper
1 teaspoon tomato paste
2 tablespoons flour
2 cups beef or chicken stock
3 tablespoons port wine
1 small bay leaf
Juice of 2 oranges
Skinned sections of 2
  oranges
1 tablespoon currant jelly*

1. Mince carrot, onion, mushrooms, and garlic. Shred orange peel.
2. Trim as much fat off duck as possible. Melt butter in a large skillet. When it is hot, brown duck, skin side first, until golden brown. This should take about 10 minutes. Remove to a casserole or heavy pot.
3. Pour off all but 2 tablespoonfuls of fat from skillet. Add vegetables, garlic, orange peel, parsley, salt, and pepper. Cook slowly 5 minutes, stirring occasionally.
4. Remove skillet from fire, and add tomato paste and flour. Stir until blended. Add stock and port. Replace skillet on burner, stir until smooth, and bring to boil.
5. Pour sauce over duck; add bay leaf. Cook slowly, covered, until tender, about 1¾ hours.
6. While duck cooks, squeeze oranges. Skin 2 other oranges and remove sections. When duck is tender, remove it to a hot serving dish.
7. Strain sauce into a clean saucepan. Skin off fat. There may be as much as ¾ to 1 cup of fat. Boil down gravy over medium heat to about 1 cup. Reduce heat; add jelly and half of orange juice. Stir to melt jelly. Add more seasoning if it is needed, and remaining orange juice to taste. Return duck to sauce to

warm up if necessary. Add orange sections. Arrange duck on a hot platter. Coat with some of the sauce. Garnish with orange sections.

Suggested Menu: shrimp cocktail, SOUR CREAM DUNK SAUCE; BRAISED DUCK À L'ORANGE; RICE PILAF; BRUSSELS SPROUTS SAUTÉ; TUTTI-FRUTTI FROZEN PUDDING.

✕ CASSEROLE DUCK

SERVES 3 · 2½ HOURS

A 4- or 4½-pound duck, cut into serving pieces	½ teaspoon salt or more
1 small onion	⅛ teaspoon pepper
1 large tomato	3 tablespoons brandy
1 clove garlic	3 medium-sized or 6 small potatoes
1 tablespoon oil	
2 tablespoons flour	1 tablespoon butter
½ teaspoon chopped lemon peel	1 tablespoon chopped parsley
1¼ cups chicken stock	½ pound medium-sized mushrooms
6 tablespoons sherry	1 tablespoon butter

1. Remove as much duck fat as possible. Chop onion and tomato. Mince garlic. Heat oil in a large skillet. Brown duck pieces well on both sides over brisk heat. Remove them to a casserole.

2. Pour off all but 2 tablespoons of fat. Cook onion in fat 2 minutes. Sprinkle it with flour and stir with wire whisk 1 minute. Add garlic, lemon peel, stock, and sherry; whisk constantly until it comes to a boil. Season with salt and pepper. Pour sauce over duck. Add tomato and bring to a boil. Heat brandy slightly in a small pan; ignite with lighted match; immediately pour it over duck. Cover and cook slowly until it is tender,

about 1¾ to 2 hours. Baste occasionally. After 1½ hours correct seasoning, adding more salt and pepper if they are needed.

3. A half-hour before duck is done, boil potatoes in jackets. Drain, steam, peel, and toss them in butter in a pan until butter melts and coats them. Chop parsley and add. Sauté whole mushrooms in butter in a separate pan 5 or 6 minutes, seasoning them as they cook.

4. Remove cooked duck to a hot serving platter. Skim off fat from sauce. Strain hot sauce over duck. Border platter with potatoes and mushrooms.

A fine dish with a delectable gravy. Be sure to skim off most of the fat; there is often as much as 1 cup of fat. Use an enamel-lined cast-iron pot, if you have one, or any heavy pot.

Suggested Menu: ANGELS ON HORSEBACK; CASSEROLE DUCK; PARSLEY POTATOES; sautéed sliced mushrooms; celery julienne and black olives on shredded lettuce, ENGLISH SALAD DRESS-ING; ALMOND SOUFFLÉ PUDDING, BLACK RASPBERRY SAUCE.

⅄ MARINATED DUCK

SERVES 3 · MARINATING 5 TO 6 HOURS OR OVERNIGHT
PREPARATION 2½ HOURS

A 4½-pound duck cut into serving pieces	2 cups dry red wine
	6 tablespoons brandy
½ teaspoon salt	1 tablespoon olive oil
¼ teaspoon pepper	2 tablespoons flour
⅛ teaspoon thyme	1 clove garlic
2 small onions	½ pound whole mushrooms
2 sprigs parsley	1 tablespoon butter
1 bay leaf	1 tablespoon chopped parsley

1. Remove as much fat as possible from duck. Rub duck pieces with mixture of salt, pepper, and thyme. Slice onions thinly.

Combine them with parsley, bay leaf, wine, and brandy. Marinate duck in mixture 5 or 6 hours or overnight, in refrigerator.

2. Drain duck parts thoroughly, and dry them. Heat oil in a skillet and when it is hot, cook duck quickly until it is well browned.

3. Strain marinade. Pour 1¼ cups marinade into a casserole or heavy saucepan, and heat. Dilute flour with ¼ cup cold marinade and add to casserole, stirring constantly until mixture boils. Add duck and garlic. Cover and cook slowly 1¼ hours.

4. Skim off fat, season with additional salt and pepper if they are needed, and cook slowly until duck is tender, about 30 minutes or more.

5. Sauté mushrooms in hot butter. Add to duck and cook 5 minutes. Chop parsley. Serve duck, sprinkled with parsley, in the casserole or on a hot platter.

Suggested Menu: SHERRIED CHEESE PÂTÉ on Melba toast; MARINATED DUCK; BOILED RICE, or RICE PILAF; BRAISED RED CABBAGE; lettuce salad, FRENCH DRESSING; RASPBERRY-PEACH SHERBET.

FISH AND SEAFOOD,
PLAIN AND FANCY

OR best results, always try to obtain fresh fish and seafood. I have prepared these recipes often with fresh and frozen fish. Where the latter is indicated, the results will be good.

To prepare fresh fish, rinse it in a cold water bath with the juice of half a lemon. Don't soak it. If solidly frozen, fish takes approximately 5 to 6 hours to thaw out in the refrigerator. At room temperature, the time may be halved. Slow thawing is preferable as the flavour is better retained. Shrimp, however, need not be completely thawed. Place them under cold running water for a few seconds to remove the icy glaze, and they are ready to be cooked.

Cooking in fat is probably the most common method of fish cookery. When butter or a combination of butter and oil is used, frying is an excellent method for cooking small fish or slices of large ones. Dip them in lightly seasoned flour, in slightly beaten egg, and in breadcrumbs. Press the coating down to make it stick. For a professional touch, crisscross fish with the dull edge of a knife before frying it in a little fat until it is crisp and done. Or soak fish in slightly salted milk and roll it in flour before frying. For a real treat, fresh-water fishermen need only

59

dip their cleaned sliced perch, pickerel, or bass in cornmeal, sprinkle it with a little salt and a lot of black pepper, and fry it quickly in hot butter.

Cooking fish in liquid often has less satisfactory results. In order to preserve its fine delicate flavour, fish should be steamed, never boiled. Oil a trivet or rack and place it in a steamer, skillet, or pot that just fits the fish. Lay the fish on the rack one layer deep. Pour in a small amount of court bouillon or seasoned water. If you are steaming fillets or slices, liquid should barely touch them. A whole fish should be no more than half or two-thirds submerged. Cover and slowly bring to a boil. Lower heat and steam fish until it flakes easily with a fork. Baste occasionally. Do not turn fish. Lift it out with the rack. From the time the liquid boils, a fillet should require about 2 to 5 minutes' steaming, depending upon its thickness; a one-inch thick fish about 6 to 8 minutes; a two-inch one about 10 to 15 minutes. Save the broth for a sauce. Serve the fish on a hot platter with a sauce—Béchamel, Velouté, Aurore, Mornay, or Hollandaise (see chapter on sauces).

ⅹ COURT BOUILLON
WITH LEMON JUICE OR VINEGAR

FOR SHELLFISH, SALMON, TROUT · 25 MINUTES

1 *carrot*	3 *sprigs parsley*
1 *small onion*	½ *small bay leaf*
1 *celery rib*	¼ *teaspoon salt*
1½ *cups water*	Pinch *thyme*
1 *tablespoon lemon juice or vinegar*	2 *peppercorns*

1. Slice carrot thinly; mince onion and celery.
2. Place all ingredients, except peppercorns, in a saucepan. Boil gently 10 to 15 minutes.
3. Add peppercorns and cook 10 minutes.
4. Strain.

❧ COURT BOUILLON WITH WHITE WINE

FOR FRESH-WATER FISH

Substitute ¼ cup dry white wine for the lemon juice or vinegar in above recipe. Proceed in the same way.

❧ SEASONED WATER

FOR SALT-WATER FISH

Combine 2 cups water and ½ teaspoon salt and cook fish as in recipe.

Liquid in which large whole fish is to be steamed should be cold at beginning of cooking process. Liquid should be warm for fillets; hot for sliced fish, lobster, and shrimp.

❧ COLD SALMON, MAYONNAISE CAPER SAUCE

SERVES 6 TO 8 · 1½ HOURS

A 3-pound salmon steak (or salmon slices ½-inch thick)
Court bouillon with lemon juice
1 cup French mayonnaise
2 tablespoons capers, drained
Lettuce
6 or 8 small tomatoes filled with cucumber salad (optional)

1. Prepare a COURT BOUILLON WITH LEMON JUICE, using enough water to cover fish to a depth of three-quarters its thickness. Strain.

2. Wrap salmon in cheesecloth to preserve shape, and lower it into hot broth. Or place it unwrapped on a thoroughly greased rack or trivet in a steamer or pan that just fits. Bring broth slowly to simmering point. Cover and simmer until fish is tender or flakes easily with fork. Allow about 15 minutes

61

per pound for thick steak and 5 or 6 minutes for half-inch slices. Do not permit liquid to boil, as the delicate flavour of the salmon will be destroyed. Let fish cool in broth.

3. One hour before serving, remove fish from broth and let drain in refrigerator.

4. Combine FRENCH MAYONNAISE and capers. Chill.

5. To serve salmon, remove wrapping. You may skin fish if you desire but it is not necessary. Centre salmon on a platter. Tuck in some lettuce leaves as a garnish. Pour some of the sauce over the fish, allowing some pink to show through. Surround with tomatoes filled with CUCUMBER SALAD if you wish.

A really good dish for a buffet supper. The slices are easier to serve than the steak. Other good garnishes are marinated sliced beets or hard-boiled eggs stuffed with cucumber and anchovy.

⅍ SALMON TIMBALES, QUICK TOMATO SAUCE
SERVES 4 TO 6 · 1 TO 1¼ HOURS

1 *pound cooked or tinned salmon*	3 *large eggs, separated*
⅔ *cup fine fresh bread-crumbs*	2 *teaspoons lemon juice*
	¾ *teaspoon salt*
	⅛ *teaspoon white pepper*
¼ *cup melted butter*	1 to 1½ *cups tomato sauce*

1. Grease well 6 custard cups (half-cup size) with butter. Have ready a steamer or large pot with a rack, and enough boiling water to reach two thirds up sides of moulds.

2. Drain salmon. Crumb bread with fingers. Combine both with butter, egg yolks, lemon juice, salt, and pepper. Mix well together. Beat egg whites very stiffly and fold in.

3. Fill cups ⅔ full of mixture. Cover with aluminium foil, pressing it down snugly. Place cups on rack in pot. Bring water to a boil, then reduce heat and simmer 40 to 50 minutes, covered.

4. While timbales cook, prepare sauce.

5. When you think timbales are done, insert knife in one of them. If it emerges dry, remove timbales from pot. Unmould timbales. Serve with hot sauce.

✕ QUICK TOMATO SAUCE

$1\frac{1}{2}$ CUPS · 25 MINUTES

1 *tablespoon onion*
$\frac{1}{2}$ *garlic clove*
1 *tomato*
$2\frac{1}{2}$ *tablespoons butter*
$2\frac{1}{2}$ *tablespoons flour*

2 *heaped tablespoons tomato*
   paste
$1\frac{1}{2}$ *cups water*
$\frac{3}{4}$ *teaspoon salt*
Pinch pepper
$\frac{1}{2}$ *teaspoon sugar*

1. Mince onion and garlic. Mince tomato.

2. Melt 2 tablespoons butter in a small saucepan. Sauté onion and garlic slowly 3 or 4 minutes. Blend in flour and tomato paste with wire whisk. Add water, salt, pepper, sugar, and bring to boil, stirring constantly with whisk. Add minced tomato. Cook over low heat 10 minutes.

3. Strain sauce into another pan, pressing pulp through strainer into sauce. Stir in remaining half-tablespoon of butter, bit by bit. Reheat if necessary, but don't reboil. Serve hot.

This makes a good summer luncheon or supper dish for unexpected guests, as you are apt to have the ingredients at hand.

Suggested Menu: CREAM OF CARROT SOUP; SALMON TIMBALES, QUICK TOMATO SAUCE; julienne or mashed potatoes; salad of beets, cucumbers, celery julienne, MUSTARD CREAM DRESSING (see CELERY SALAD); tinned greengages with ginger (see MORE WAYS WITH FRUIT).

⚰ FISH FRICADELLES

SERVES 4 · 40 MINUTES

1½ cups cold water
¼ teaspoon salt
1½ pounds fresh fillets of
  sole
Strip of lemon peel, ½ by 1
  inch
¼ teaspoon minced parsley
½ teaspoon minced fresh dill
2 egg yolks, unbeaten
3 tablespoons fine bread-
  crumbs

2 tablespoons melted butter
⅛ teaspoon pepper
4 tablespoons butter
2 tablespoons flour
1½ cups reserved fish stock
3 tablespoons port
Dash cayenne
½ to 1 teaspoon lemon juice
¾ chicken bouillon cube

1. Add salt to water in a saucepan and heat. When it is warm place fillets in pot gently. Slowly bring water to a boil. Simmer 4 or 5 minutes until fish flakes easily. Remove fillets, well drained, to chopping bowl. Strain fish liquor and reserve.

2. Mince lemon peel, parsley, and dill. Add to fish. Chop these together 2 or 3 minutes. Add egg yolks, breadcrumbs, melted butter, and pepper; mix together. It should be a soft mixture.

3. Melt 2 tablespoons butter in a skillet over medium-low heat. Shape fish mixture into 1½-inch balls and brown them quickly on both sides. Don't crowd pan or they will be difficult to turn. Remove them to serving dish.

4. Melt remaining butter in saucepan. Blend in flour with wire whisk. Add fish stock, wine, cayenne, lemon juice, and bouillon cube. Stir constantly with whisk until sauce boils. Simmer 3 minutes. Place fish balls in sauce and simmer 5 minutes.

5. Serve hot with a little of the sauce.

An excellent luncheon or supper dish as well as a fine first course. This recipe makes about 18 fish balls. As an appetizer,

2 would be sufficient for each serving, with slices of cucumber and tomato.

Suggested Menu: CABBAGE SOUP; FISH FRICADELLES; boiled macaroni with melted butter, grated Parmesan and Gruyère cheese; GREEN BEANS OREGANO with cucumber slices; PRUNE WHIP.

✂ FILLETS OF SOLE IN CHEESE SAUCE

SERVES 3 TO 4 · 25 MINUTES
PLUS THAWING

1 *pound fresh or frozen fillets
   of sole*

CHEESE SAUCE

1 *teaspoon chopped onion*	2 *tablespoons sherry*
½ *teaspoon chopped parsley*	⅛ *teaspoon salt*
½ *teaspoon chopped fresh*	*Dash cayenne*
dill	*Dash Tabasco*
2 *tablespoons butter*	¼ *cup grated Parmesan*
1 *tablespoon flour*	*cheese*
1 *cup milk*	
1½ *tablespoons butter*	*A few sprigs parsley for*
Salt and pepper to taste	*garnish*
Paprika	

1. Thaw fish completely if frozen.
2. Chop onion, parsley, and dill.
3. Make cheese sauce in the top of a double boiler directly over moderate-low heat. Melt butter. Blend in flour away from heat, using wire whisk. Add milk gradually, stirring constantly with whisk. Bring to a boil. Add sherry, onion, parsley, dill, salt, cayenne, and Tabasco. Add cheese and stir until it melts. Place pan over simmering water until sauce is needed.

4. Melt butter over low heat in a large skillet. Sauté fillets 1 or 2 minutes on each side. Season with salt and pepper. Be careful not to oversalt as sherry dishes require less salt.

5. Place fish on a warm platter. Pour hot sauce over it. Dust lightly with paprika. Garnish with parsley.
Frozen sole is suited to this dish if fresh fillets are not available.

Suggested Menu: CONSOMMÉ CELESTINE; FILLETS OF SOLE IN CHEESE SAUCE; GREEN BEANS AMANDINE; shoestring potatoes; CHOPPED VEGETABLE SALAD with escarole; CHESTNUT PUDDING, COFFEE RUM SAUCE.

STEAMED WHITING IN SAUCE POULETTE

SERVES 3 TO 4 · 40 MINUTES
PLUS THAWING

1 *packet (1 pound) frozen whiting fillets*

COURT BOUILLON WITH WHITE
   WINE

SAUCE POULETTE

2 *tablespoons minced onion*	1 *teaspoon lemon juice*
2 *tablespoons minced carrot*	1 *egg yolk*
2 *tablespoons butter*	1 *teaspoon sherry (optional)*
2 *tablespoons flour*	*Salt to taste*
¾ *cup reserved fish stock*	*Dash cayenne*
½ *cup milk*	

1 *tablespoon chopped parsley or dill*

1. Thaw fish.

2. Mince onion and carrot for poulette sauce.

3. Make COURT BOUILLON WITH WHITE WINE.

4. Place a greased rack in a steamer or large skillet. Pour warm court bouillon into steamer. Lay fish on rack. Do not let liquid touch fish. Bring broth slowly to boil. Cover and steam fish about 5 minutes or until it flakes easily. Lift out rack with fillets carefully. Strain stock and reserve. Return rack with fish to pan, cover and keep warm.

5. To make SAUCE POULETTE, melt butter in top of a double boiler, directly over low heat. Add onion and carrot, and cook 3 minutes. Blend in flour away from heat and stir until smooth. Add fish stock and milk, using wire whisk. Bring sauce to boil, stirring constantly. Mix in lemon juice. Place over simmering water. In a small bowl, beat egg yolk slightly. Add to it 4 tablespoons of sauce, 1 spoonful at a time. Stir this slowly into sauce. Add sherry, if desired. Season liberally with salt and cayenne.

5. Transfer fish to a hot platter. Ladle some of the sauce over it. Sprinkle with parsley or dill.

Suggested Menu: LEEK AND POTATO SOUP; STEAMED WHITING IN SAUCE POULETTE; CARROTS SAUTERNE; CUCUMBER SALAD with sliced green onions; guava jelly and cream cheese on saltine crackers.

✖ COD WITH SOUR CREAM SAUCE

SERVES 3 · 30 MINUTES
PLUS THAWING

1 *pound fresh or frozen cod*	*¼ teaspoon paprika*
fillets	*¼ teaspoon salt*
Grated rind of 1 *lemon*	*⅛ teaspoon pepper*
2 *tablespoons lemon juice*	6 *tablespoons sour cream*
2 *tablespoons chopped parsley*	2 *tablespoons capers*
1 *large onion*	*Paprika for dusting*
2 *to* 3 *tablespoons butter*	

1. Thaw fish, if it is frozen.

2. Grate lemon rind and squeeze lemon. Chop parsley. Reserve all three.

3. Slice onion thinly. Melt butter in a large skillet over low heat and brown onion lightly. Sprinkle with paprika and stir to blend.

4. Cut fish into serving portions and add. Brown them slightly 2 or 3 minutes, seasoning with salt and pepper. Turn them carefully with spatula and brown other side.

5. Add sour cream, lemon juice, grated lemon rind, 1 teaspoon of chopped parsley, and capers. Stir gently to combine. Pour sauce over fish. Cover and simmer 10 minutes or until fish flakes when touched with fork. Do not overcook.

6. Serve with a sprinkling of paprika and remaining parsley. This recipe is ideally suited for use with frozen cod or halibut, but thaw fish first.

Suggested Menu: salmon roe on thin pumpernickel bread squares, with lemon slice; COD WITH SOUR CREAM SAUCE; puréed potatoes, sprinkled with chopped chives; sliced cucumber and tomato salad with chopped fresh dill or parsley, FRENCH DRESSING with lemon juice; assorted cheeses and bowl of fruit (see CHEESE AND FRUIT FOR DESSERT).

⅛ HALIBUT SPANISH STYLE

SERVES 4 · 50 MINUTES

1 to 1½ *pounds halibut steaks*	⅛ *teaspoon pepper*
1 *large onion*	⅛ *teaspoon paprika*
3 *tablespoons butter*	1½ *teaspoons grated*
1 *tablespoon flour*	*chocolate, sweetened or*
¾ *cup hot water*	*unsweetened*
¼ *cup dry white wine*	8 *large mushrooms*
Salt to taste	1 *teaspoon lemon juice*

68

1. Mince onion. Melt butter and when it is hot, sauté onion slowly 10 minutes.

2. Blend in flour. Add hot water, wine, salt, pepper, and paprika. Stir until it comes to a boil. Add chocolate and stir until it melts. Lay fish over sauce and cook slowly until it is almost tender, about 20 to 25 minutes. Shake pan; baste occasionally.

3. Slice mushrooms. Add them with lemon juice and cook 10 minutes.

4. Serve hot with some of the sauce.

The chocolate gives the sauce an unusual colour. You might like the addition of a tiny pinch of sugar. Add a little more hot water if necessary, but it should not cover the fish.

Suggested Menu: STUFFED CARROTS; HALIBUT SPANISH STYLE; BOILED RICE; fried sliced aubergine; sliced celery and cucumber salad, FRENCH DRESSING; COLD LEMON SOUFFLÉ, FROSTED ORANGE SECTIONS.

✷ COLD BOILED LOBSTER, REMOULADE SAUCE

SERVES 2 · 1¼ HOURS

A 2½-pound lobster or two baby lobsters, 1¼ to 1½ pounds each	3 sprigs parsley
	Vinegar
	Salt
1 small onion	2 peppercorns
1 small carrot	Lettuce leaves or curly
Pinch thyme	parsley for garnish
1 small bay leaf, crushed	

1. Chop onion and carrot. Place enough cold water in a large kettle to cover lobster. Add onion, carrot, thyme, bay, parsley, and 1 tablespoon of vinegar and ½ teaspoon of salt for each cup of water. Bring to a boil. Simmer 20 minutes. Add peppercorns and simmer 10 minutes. Strain broth. Return it to

pan and bring to a rapid boil. Add lobster, head first. Boil vigorously 10 minutes. Reduce to low heat and cook 10 minutes. Let lobster cool in broth.

2. Drain. Break off large claws. Open them with a hammer or nutcracker so that meat can be removed. With a pair of scissors, split lobster in half by slitting underside from head to tail. Remove stomach (hard sac near head) and black intestinal vein running down back of tail meat. Leave all other parts intact, including coral (roe) and green (liver) parts. Arrange lobster on a platter with a claw on each side. Border with shredded lettuce or parsley sprigs.

3. Serve at room temperature or chilled. Pass sauce.

⅄ REMOULADE SAUCE

MAKES 1 CUP · 5 MINUTES

½ tablespoon capers
1 tablespoon chopped sweet
    or dill cucumber pickle
1 teaspoon chopped parsley
¼ teaspoon dried tarragon

½ tablespoon prepared
    mustard
1 cup mayonnaise, preferably
    FRENCH MAYONNAISE

1. Drain capers and pickles and chop fine with parsley.
2. Combine all ingredients. Stir until well blended.
3. Let stand 1 hour to blend flavours.
   Good with cold meat and chicken as well as lobster.
   Prepare sauce while court bouillon cooks. The salad suggested below is simply a combination of chilled cooked and uncooked vegetables, such as potatoes, green beans, peas, asparagus tips, celery, carrots, parsley. Or use frozen mixed vegetables.

Suggested Menu: cream of cauliflower soup (see SOME CHOICE SOUPS, introduction); COLD BOILED LOBSTER, REMOULADE SAUCE; mixed vegetable salad, FRENCH DRESSING with lemon juice; PEACH MELBA.

ꙮ CRAB JAMBALAYA

SERVES 4 · 1 HOUR
PLUS THAWING

2 *cups freshly cooked crab meat*   3 *tablespoons butter*
   or 2 packets frozen crab $\frac{1}{4}$ *teaspoon salt*
   meat, thawed and drained   *Pinch pepper*
1 *cup raw rice*   *Pinch cayenne*
1 *medium-sized onion*   1 *teaspoon chili powder or*
1 *small clove garlic*   *more to taste*
2 *medium-sized tomatoes*

1. Boil rice and let it steam, covered, over burner, with heat off. (See BOILED RICE.)
2. Chop onion and garlic. Skin and mince tomatoes. Cube crab meat.
3. Melt 1 tablespoon of butter in a saucepan. When it is hot, sauté onion and garlic 3 or 4 minutes. Add tomatoes and crush them with back of spoon; blend with onion. Simmer 10 minutes.
4. Melt 2 tablespoons of butter in a separate pan and sauté crab meat 2 or 3 minutes. Combine with onion-tomato mixture, salt, pepper, cayenne, chili powder, and rice. Cover and cook slowly 15 minutes, stirring occasionally. Serve in a deep dish.

Suggested Menu: CHICKEN GUMBO SOUP; CRAB JAMBALAYA; PURÉED CARROTS; FRENCH FRITTERS, APRICOT-ORANGE SAUCE.

ꙮ CRAB SAUTÉ

SERVES 4 · 30 MINUTES

2 *cups cooked crab meat (or*   2 *medium carrots*
   2 *packets frozen cooked*   4 *tablespoons butter*
   crab meat)   *Salt and pepper to taste*
1 *cup raw rice*   *Dash cayenne*
1 *large onion*   6 *black olives*

1. If you are using frozen crab meat, thaw it before cooking. Drain meat well and cut into cubes.

2. Cook rice. (See RICE PILAF.)

3. Chop onion and carrots finely and combine them. Melt 2 tablespoons of butter over low heat in a large frying-pan. Add onion and carrots and cook 5 minutes. Add remaining 2 tablespoons of butter. Mix in crab meat and seasoning to taste. Sauté long enough to heat crab meat through.

4. Stone olives and slice them. Mix with cooked rice. Cook 2 or 3 minutes. Serve in a deep dish.

   Frozen crab meat is excellent in this recipe. Leftover cooked rice may be used too, but it should be reheated before adding olives. This delicate, subtly flavoured dish will pique the most jaded appetite.

Suggested Menu: SOUP ST. GERMAIN; CRAB SAUTÉ; CREAMED SPINACH; mixed red and white cabbage salad, FRENCH DRESSING with extra tablespoon of lemon juice; HOMEMADE CREAM CHEESE with preserved ginger.

⅍ SHRIMP CURRY

SERVES 3 TO 4 · 1 TO 1¼ HOURS

1½ pounds raw, unshelled
  shrimp
1 small onion
½ carrot
1 rib celery
1 clove garlic
1 large cucumber
1¼ cups hot water
½ teaspoon salt
1 tablespoon lemon juice
4 tablespoons butter
1 tablespoon curry powder

¾ teaspoon salt
Good pinch pepper
1½ tablespoons flour
¾ cup milk
4 tablespoons shredded
  coconut, fresh or dried
1 small stick cinnamon
2 cloves stuck into 1 shrimp
½ teaspoon sugar
1 teaspoon lemon juice or
  more to taste
1 cup raw rice

1. Coarsely chop onion, carrot, and celery. Mince garlic. Peel cucumber; cut in halves lengthwise; remove seeds; slice into 1-inch chunks.

2. Rinse shrimps quickly in cold water, and drain. Place them in hot water with salt and lemon juice. Bring to a boil; cook slowly 3 minutes. Strain. Save ¾ cup of liquor.

3. Melt 2 tablespoons of butter in a saucepan. Add onion, carrot, celery, and garlic. Cook slowly 5 minutes. Stir in curry, salt, and pepper; cook 3 minutes. Add flour, away from heat, blending until smooth. Whisk in milk and reserved liquor, and bring to a boil, stirring constantly. Add coconut, cucumber, cinnamon, and sugar. Stick cloves into shrimp to keep track of them. Cook slowly 20 to 25 minutes; stir occasionally. Add lemon juice.

4. While sauce cooks, make rice (see BOILED RICE) and keep hot.

5. Shell and devein shrimp. Rinse quickly in cold water. Drain and dry with paper towels. Sauté shrimp in 2 tablespoons of hot butter 3 or 4 minutes.

6. Remove cloves from sauce. Combine sauce and shrimp just long enough to heat shrimp through. Pile shrimp with sauce in centre of a hot platter and border with rice.

Curry requires something refreshing and tart along with it.

Suggested Menu: CHICKEN AND HAM PUFFS; SHRIMP CURRY; RICE PILAF WITH RAISINS AND ALMONDS; CUCUMBERS MAÎTRE D'HÔTEL; grapefruit and orange sections and watercress, FRENCH DRESSING with lemon juice; TIPSY TRIFLES, vanilla ice cream.

❧ RISOTTO WITH SHRIMP

SERVES 4 · 1¼ HOURS

1½ *pounds shrimp*
1 *medium carrot*
2 *small onions*
2½ *cups cold water*
½ *small bay leaf*
3 *sprigs parsley*
1 *teaspoon salt*
1 *tablespoon oil*
1 *cup raw long grain rice*

Salt and white pepper to
taste
½ *cup flour*
¼ *teaspoon salt*
⅛ *teaspoon white pepper*
2 *cups oil for deep frying, or*
   4 *tablespoons oil for shallow*
frying

1. Shell, devein, rinse, and drain shrimp. Rinse shells and save.
2. Mince carrot and 1 onion. Add these to water with shrimp shells, bay leaf, parsley, and salt. Bring to a boil. Cook slowly 30 minutes and strain stock, reserving it.
3. Mince second onion. Heat oil in a skillet over low heat. Add onion and rice, and cook uncovered 5 minutes until they are lightly coloured, but not brown. Turn frequently with a spatula so that rice does not burn or brown. Remove skillet from heat and add slowly 2 cups reserved hot stock. Stir, return to heat, and season with salt and pepper to taste. Bring to a boil. Cover, reduce to low heat, and cook 15 minutes. Stock should be almost completely absorbed. Turn off heat, but keep pan over burner. Fluff up rice with 2 forks. Cover and let rice steam.
4. While rice cooks, do shrimp. Combine flour, salt, and pepper. Dip shrimp in flour. Either fry in hot deep oil or sauté in hot shallow oil until golden brown. Drain. Fold shrimp into cooked steaming rice and allow flavours to blend, covered, 5 minutes.
5. Serve immediately on hot plates.

Suggested Menu: cream cheese and caviar on toast triangles (see CREAM CHEESE-RED CAVIAR CANAPES); RISOTTO WITH SHRIMP; sautéed mushrooms and tomatoes; CUCUMBER AND GREEN PEPPER SALAD, TUTTI-FRUTTI FROZEN PUDDING.

APPETIZERS AND HORS D'OEUVRES
FOR COCKTAILS AND DINNER

✴   ✴   ✴   ✴   ✴   ✴   ✴   ✴

APPETIZERS and hors d'oeuvres are intended, in the main, to accompany the before-dinner drink, but they may be served at the table without drinks. Two or three appetizers may be offered at the same time, but they should not be overdone; they are intended to whet rather than diminish the appetite. A variety of chilled crisp raw vegetables, with or without a dunk sauce, is universally appealing in warm weather and is always attractive to people who are dieting. Appetizers and hors d'oeuvres are usually served on or with toast triangles or "fingers", Melba toast, thin pumpernickel squares, bread sticks, or plain crackers.

Any of the heartier recipes in this section may be used as the principal course of a light luncheon. Try the meat salad, cold boiled salmon, fish and beef fricadelles, stuffed eggs or tomatoes, chicken and ham puffs, and shrimp dishes.

✄ HERRING SALAD

SERVES 8 TO 10 · PREPARATION 30 MINUTES
CHILLING SEVERAL HOURS OR OVERNIGHT

2 jars herring fillets (16 ounces in all) in vinegar or wine
1⅓ cups cooked veal or beef
1⅓ cups cooked beets
1⅓ cups cooked potatoes, not too soft
1⅓ cups raw apple, peeled
6 pickled sweet gherkins
½ cup chopped onion (optional)

4 eggs
6 tablespoons bland oil
2 tablespoons wine vinegar
6 tablespoons dry white wine
¼ to ½ teaspoon pepper
¼ to ½ teaspoon dry mustard
2 teaspoons sugar
Salt to taste

1. Drain herring. Remove any bones that are in herring. Discard any onions. Mince herring.
2. Cube next 5 ingredients. Chop onion. Combine these with herring. Hard-boil eggs.
3. Place next 7 ingredients in a jar and shake well. Pour over salad. Turn with 2 forks to mix.
4. Chill salad and hard-boiled eggs several hours or, preferably, overnight.
5. To serve, pile up salad in bowl or turn out of mould on to platter. Slice eggs for border, and edge bowl or platter with lettuce.

The seasoning of this type of salad is so dependent upon the nature of the herring that I suggest proceeding with caution. Taste again after salad has mellowed, to check need for additional seasoning. Rye bread or pumpernickel should be served with the salad.

✻ FLEMISH SALAD

SERVES 4 TO 6 · PREPARATION 15 MINUTES
REFRIGERATION SEVERAL HOURS

2 tablespoons Bermuda onion	3 tablespoons oil
¾ cup cooked potatoes	1 tablespoon wine vinegar
*½ cup salt herring fillets	⅛ teaspoon white pepper
1 tablespoon chopped parsley	1½ cups endive
and fresh chervil combined,	Salt to taste
or 1 tablespoon chopped	4 to 6 tomato slices
parsley	

* *Use any kind of mild salt herring, pickled or plain.*

1. Chop onion. Cut potatoes into matchlike strips. Dice herring and combine with potatoes and onion.
2. Chop parsley and chervil. Combine these with oil, vinegar, pepper. Pour over herring mixture. Toss. Refrigerate for several hours to blend flavours.
3. Immediately before serving, shred endive and add. Taste to see if salt is needed. Serve each portion on a thin tomato slice.

✻ ANCHOVY AND PIMENTO SALAD

SERVES 4 TO 6 · 20 MINUTES

4 ounces tinned anchovy	Lettuce leaves
fillets	2 tablespoons lemon juice
2 hard-boiled eggs	⅛ teaspoon freshly ground
1 small white onion	black pepper
1 tablespoon minced parsley	⅛ teaspoon oregano
3 tinned pimentos	

1. Chop egg whites finely. Push yolks through sieve. Mince onion and parsley. Cut pimentos into strips same size as anchovies.

2. Drain off oil from anchovies and save it. Run cold water through anchovies to wash off some of salt. Drain.

3. Shred enough lettuce leaves to make a bed for anchovies. Separate fillets and place them in a neat row on lettuce. Lay pimento strips across fillets to form lattice.

4. Combine oil from tins with lemon juice, onion, and pepper. Pour dressing over anchovies. Sprinkle with oregano. Top with chopped egg whites and sieved yolks, arranged in alternating pattern. Dust with minced parsley.

5. Serve at room temperature or slightly chilled with Melba toast, bread sticks, or thinly sliced French or Italian bread.

⚓ ANGELS ON HORSEBACK

SERVES 4 · 25 MINUTES

12 *oysters, fresh*	1 *lemon, quartered*
Juice of 1 *lemon*	6 *bacon slices*
2 *tablespoons chopped*	1 *tablespoon butter*
parsley	*Cayenne*
3 *slices white toast*	

1. Marinate oysters in lemon juice 10 minutes. Chop parsley. Cut each of 3 toast slices into 4 triangles. Dip lemon quarters into parsley. Cut bacon slices into halves crosswise. Have ready a hot platter.

2. Drain and dry oysters. Wrap bacon piece around each one and fasten with toothpick.

3. Melt butter in a skillet. When it is very hot, add wrapped oysters and cook over brisk heat until bacon is crisp. Turn to cook other side. This should take no longer than 5 minutes. Place oysters on paper towels to drain.

4. Set oysters on toast triangles. Dust them lightly with cayenne.

Arrange them on a platter with lemon wedges. Serve immediately.

A good appetizer or hors d'oeuvre, requiring little preparation.

❧ MOULES MARINIÈRE · Mussels Sailor's Style

SERVES 6 TO 8 · 1 HOUR

4 *dozen mussels*	2 *chopped shallots or* 1
1 *onion*	*tablespoon chopped onion*
1 *carrot*	1 *cup dry white wine*
1 *rib celery*	3 *tablespoons butter*
2 *sprigs parsley*	1 *tablespoon cream*
1 *small bay leaf, crushed*	¼ *teaspoon lemon juice*
Pinch salt and pepper	*Salt and pepper to taste*
1 *cup cold water*	3 *tablespoons chopped parsley*
1 *clove garlic*	

1. Wash mussels in several waters. Scrub them thoroughly. Cut off black tuft and beard.
2. Chop onion, carrot, celery, and parsley. Place these in a steamer with insert. Add crushed bay leaf, salt, pepper, mussels. Pour in water. Cover tightly; bring to a boil and let mussels steam over high heat only until shells open. Transfer mussels to a hot dish, pouring off into pot any juice in shells. Remove 1 shell from each mussel.
3. Strain broth into another pot, leaving sandy residue at bottom.
4. Mince garlic and add it, with chopped shallots or onion, to wine in a small pan. Boil quickly to reduce wine to ⅓ cup. Add this to the strained broth with butter, cream, and lemon juice, and salt and pepper to taste.
5. Return mussels in shells to broth. Heat them quickly a few seconds. Serve them hot in bowls with a little broth, sprinkled with parsley.

Plain or toasted crusty French bread or crackers go with this. Don't try to make the dish unless you have a steamer with a rack. So much time is consumed just moving mussels from pot to dish to pot. You may make smaller quantities in an ordinary pan. Use half as much water and wine, onion, carrot, butter, and chopped parsley. This recipe also makes a fine main dish, with French bread and a green salad.

CURRIED LOBSTER ON TOAST

SERVES 4 TO 5 · 20 MINUTES

2 *or* 3 *slices buttered toast, cut diagonally in half*
1 *medium-sized cucumber, cut into sticks*
FRENCH DRESSING, *made with lemon juice*
1 *tablespoon chopped fresh dill or parsley*

1 *cup cooked fresh, frozen (defrosted), or tinned lobster*
3 *tablespoons butter*
2 *teaspoons sherry*
$\frac{1}{4}$ *teaspoon curry or more to taste*
Good pinch dry mustard

1. Prepare toast and cucumber sticks. Marinate sticks in FRENCH DRESSING. Chop dill or parsley.
2. Mince lobster. Sauté it in hot butter 3 or 4 minutes until it is warmed. Stir in sherry and cook 30 seconds. Add curry and mustard; mix and cook 30 seconds.
3. Serve lobster on toast triangles. Garnish with cucumber sticks, sprinkled with dill or parsley.

SHRIMP VINAIGRETTE

SERVES 5 TO 6 · PREPARATION 25 TO 30 MINUTES
CHILLING 3 HOURS

1 *pound medium-sized shrimp*

VINAIGRETTE SAUCE FOR FISH

½ *cup salad oil*	1 *teaspoon chopped chives*
1 *tablespoon wine vinegar*	1 *teaspoon chopped onion*
2 *tablespoons lemon juice*	1 *teaspoon chopped parsley*
1 *teaspoon prepared mustard*	½ *teaspoon salt*
1 *tablespoon capers, well* *drained*	*Few drops Tabasco*

Soup greens: 1 *carrot,* 1 *rib* *celery,* 3 *sprigs celery leaf,* 1 *parsnip (optional)*	1½ *cups water* *Shredded lettuce*

1. To make VINAIGRETTE SAUCE, combine in a jar the ingredients listed. Shake well.

2. Boil soup greens gently in water. Shell, devein, and rinse shrimp. Cook 5 minutes in boiling broth. Let them cool in it.

3. Drain them well. Mix with prepared sauce. Chill well.

4. Before serving, shred lettuce. Mix salad again and place individual portions on plates with lettuce.

You may garnish each plate with slices of cucumber and tomato. Pass Melba toast or plain crackers.

✄ Variation

For SHRIMP SALAD, follow Steps 1, 2 and 3, adding 1 thinly sliced celery rib. Pile salad in the centre of a platter on a bed of shredded lettuce or romaine when ready to serve. Border with 2 quartered, hard-boiled eggs and 2 sliced tomatoes. Peel and slice an avocado, dip it all over in FRENCH DRESSING, and arrange in border. Sprinkle a little dressing over eggs and tomatoes. Hard finger rolls, crusty white bread, and bread sticks all go well with the salad. This recipe will serve 3 or 4 as a luncheon or supper dish.

⅄ SAUTÉED SHRIMP

SERVES 8 · PREPARATION 30 TO 40 MINUTES
MARINATING 30 MINUTES

2 *pounds jumbo shrimp*	⅛ *teaspoon pepper*
2 *teaspoons Worcester*	1 *large egg*
Sauce	1 *tablespoon salad oil*
2 *teaspoons lemon juice*	½ *cup fine breadcrumbs*
1½ *teaspoons dry mustard*	3 *or 4 tablespoons butter*

1. Shell and devein shrimp. Rinse quickly and dry.
2. Combine Worcester Sauce, lemon juice, mustard, and pepper. Marinate shrimp in mixture 30 minutes at least. Move around once to moisten all over.
3. Beat egg and oil slightly. Dip shrimp, undrained, into egg, then in breadcrumbs.
4. Melt butter in large frying-pan over medium-low heat. When it is hot, raise heat slightly and cook shrimp 2 minutes on each side.
5. Serve with DIPPING SAUCE.

⅄ DIPPING SAUCE

MAKES 1½ CUPS · 5 MINUTES

1 *cup chicken or beef broth,*	4 *tablespoons soy sauce*
fresh or tinned	2 *teaspoons prepared*
2 *teaspoons sugar*	*horseradish*

1. Heat broth to boiling point. Turn off heat and dissolve sugar in broth.
2. Mix in soy sauce and horseradish.
3. Serve hot.
   These shrimp are tasty hot; good cold. As an hors d'oeuvre, several shrimp may be placed on individual plates with a garnish of finely shredded romaine or a parsley spray. Serve sauce

in tiny bowls. For main luncheon or supper dish, serve with
BOILED RICE or RICE PILAF.

⅍ FISH IN VINEGAR-RAISIN SAUCE

SERVES 8 · PREPARATION 20 MINUTES
MARINATING 1 HOUR OR MORE · CHILLING SEVERAL HOURS

1 *pound fresh fillet of*
  sole
2 *tablespoons flour*
¼ *teaspoon salt*
2 *tablespoons olive oil*
1 *large onion*
2 *tablespoons raisins*

2 *tablespoons pine nuts*
½ *cup mild wine vinegar*
Dash Tabasco
1 *medium-sized tomato*
Lettuce
Cucumber slices

1. Dust fish lightly with flour and salt. Heat oil in a pan over
   moderate heat. Sauté fish about 1½ minutes on each side.
   Remove it to a large bowl.
2. Chop onion and sauté in same pan with raisins and nuts.
   Cook 4 to 5 minutes without browning onions.
3. Separate fish into large flakes. Add onion mixture, vinegar,
   and Tabasco sauce. Mix gently so as not to mash fish. Let
   marinate in refrigerator 1 hour. Drain off any unabsorbed
   vinegar. Refrigerate several hours more or overnight.
4. One hour before serving, seed and chop tomato and add to
   fish. Mix. Serve on individual plates with shredded lettuce
   and cucumber slices.
   Frozen fillets may be used, but thaw them before cooking.
   The amount of vinegar given may not be enough for your
   taste. Add more discreetly if desired, as the fish should have a
   mild but definitely vinegary taste. The addition of a little oil
   will correct a too acid result. Thinly-sliced toasted Italian or
   French bread, pumpernickel, or plain unsalted crackers are
   fine with the fish.

⅍ LIVER PÂTÉ

MAKES ABOUT 2 CUPS · PREPARATION 15 TO 20 MINUTES
CHILLING 2 TO 3 HOURS

1 *pound liverwurst*
4 *tablespoons butter, softened*
  at room temperature
1 *tablespoon lemon juice*
2 *to 3 teaspoons Bourbon or*
  other whisky
1 *small onion*
⅛ *teaspoon dried thyme*
⅛ *teaspoon black pepper*

2 *to 4 tablespoons finely-*
  chopped parsley
2 *tablespoons finely-chopped*
  fresh chives
About 12 *small black or*
  green olives, sliced
Toast fingers
Crackers

1. Mash liverwurst in a bowl until soft and workable. Blend in softened butter and mix until well combined. Using an electric blender for this step produces an especially smooth result.
2. Stir in lemon juice and whisky. Grate onion into bowl. Powder thyme with fingers and add with pepper. Add salt only if needed, as liverwurst is usually well salted.
3. Butter 3 small moulds. Pack and press pâté into them, making sure to leave no spaces. Chill thoroughly for at least 2 or 3 hours. Overnight is better.
4. Run knife down sides of moulds and carefully turn out.
5. Chop parsley finely, and chives if available. Slice olives thinly. Roll one mould of pâté, sides and top, in parsley; a second in chives; trim the third with sliced olives. Serve on a platter encircled with unbuttered toast fingers, and/or crackers.

This pâté may also be served in a bowl, sprinkled with parsley and accompanied by toast and crackers, but it deserves the attractive and simple setting described above. Don't be misled by the length of the recipe. Try it!

⚜ CHICKEN LIVER PÂTÉ

SERVES 4 TO 6 · PREPARATION 25 TO 30 MINUTES ·
CHILLING 3 HOURS

2 eggs	⅛ teaspoon pepper
2 tablespoons minced onion	2 tablespoons chicken fat or
2 tablespoons chicken fat or	mayonnaise
butter	Thinly-sliced rye bread or
4 chicken livers	pumpernickel, or saltines
¼ teaspoon salt	6 or 8 radish roses

1. Hard-boil and shell eggs. Mince onion.
2. Melt 2 tablespoons fat or butter over medium heat in a small skillet. Sauté chicken livers until well done, seasoning them as they cook. Remove them from pan. Add more fat if necessary and cook onion without browning 2 or 3 minutes.
3. Chop liver, onion, and eggs together finely, or put them through food chopper. Blend in melted fat or mayonnaise Add more salt and pepper if needed. Chill well.
4. Remove crusts and cut bread into small squares or rounds, or use saltines. Spread these thickly with pâté. Offer with the canapés a dish of chilled radish roses (see RAW VEGETABLE PLATTER). Or serve canapés on individual plates with crisp lettuce leaves and radish roses.

If mixture seems dry, add a little more fat or mayonnaise. Use chicken fat if you have it, but mayonnaise is an acceptable substitute. Some stores stock a tiny sliced rye or pumpernickel party loaf. The size is perfect for spreads.

⚜ Variation

For AVOCADO-LIVER PÂTÉ, omit eggs and start with Step 2. Proceed with Step 3, using mayonnaise. Halve a small, well-ripened, chilled avocado and discard stone. Immediately squeeze juice of half a lemon over the fruit. Remove and mash pulp. Combine with liver pâté, 1 teaspoon of Worcester Sauce, and 1 or 2 dashes of Tabasco. The pâté should be rather highly seasoned and not dry. Taste; add a little more seasoning and mayonnaise if needed. Serve on Melba rounds or thin toast. Use up within the half-hour as avocado mixtures don't keep.

CREAM CHEESE–RED CAVIAR CANAPÉS

MAKES ABOUT 1½ CUPS · 15 MINUTES

8 ounces cream cheese
¼ cup white or Bermuda onion, chopped finely
About ¼ cup light or medium cream

4 ounces red caviar
Few drops lemon juice
Thin pumpernickel slices

1. Have cheese at room temperature.
2. Chop onion very finely.
3. Add cream to cheese and work them together with fork until blended and cheese is well softened.
4. Add onion, caviar, and lemon juice. Blend until caviar is well distributed.
5. Spread on lightly buttered thin pumpernickel squares.

A good mixture for stuffing celery ribs.

SHERRIED CHEESE PÂTÉ

MAKES ABOUT 1½ CUPS · PREPARATION 5 TO 10 MINUTES
MELLOWING 2 TO 3 DAYS

6 ounces cream cheese (2 small packets)
6 ounces Danish Blue or Roquefort cheese

6 tablespoons unsalted butter
2 teaspoons sherry or brandy
Dash cayenne

1. Have cheese and butter at room temperature.
2. Blend them together thoroughly. Blend in sherry or brandy and cayenne, using electric blender if you have one.
3. Cover tightly and let stand in refrigerator at least 2 or 3 days, to improve flavour.
4. Bring pâté to room temperature before using. Spread on thinly-sliced pumpernickel. Or pack into a bowl, top it with thin olive slices and serve with an assortment of plain crackers.

This very good spread will keep for weeks in refrigerator.

✄ Variation I

For STUFFED CELERY, increase amount of Blue or Roquefort cheese by 1 or 2 tablespoons. Proceed with Steps 1, 2, and 3. Cut off leafy parts of 1 stalk Pascal celery. Remove coarse strings with potato peeler. Cut ribs into 3-inch sections and stuff them with prepared pâté. Serve chilled on small platter with black and green olives arranged in attractive pattern.

✄ Variation II

For CELERY WHEELS, increase amount of cream cheese by 2 ounces. Omit butter, sherry, brandy, and cayenne. Blend 1 or 2 tablespoons of cream or milk into softened cheeses until they are of spreading consistency. Then add $\frac{1}{4}$ teaspoon Worcester Sauce. Taste, adding more Worcester Sauce drop by drop until flavour is quite snappy. Test by tasting a bit of celery spread with cheese mixture. Cut across unseparated stalk, 6 or $6\frac{1}{2}$ inches from root end. Detach ribs carefully, wash, dry, and fill with spread. Reconstruct stalk and fasten with string or rubber bands. Wrap in waxed paper or foil and chill several hours or overnight. To serve, cut across width of stalk into half-inch slices or wheels. Three wheels may be arranged on individual plates with small lettuce leaf and a couple of olives.

Either of these celery variations is fine on a RAW VEGETABLE PLATTER in place of celery sticks or curls. Either makes a good garnish for a crab or shrimp salad.

⚘ TUNA-PARMESAN PÂTÉ

MAKES ABOUT 1⅓ CUPS · 15 MINUTES

½ cup freshly grated
  Parmesan cheese
7 ounces tinned Italian tuna
  (tonno) in olive oil

2 or 3 tablespoons milk
3 tablespoons chopped parsley

1. Place grated cheese and fish with its oil in mortar, and pound until well mashed. Add more cheese if desired. Press through a sieve into a bowl.
2. Blend in milk a little at a time until pâté is of spreading consistency.
3. Spread on unbuttered, warm toast triangles. Sprinkle lightly with chopped parsley.

As a first course this pâté may also be served on shredded greens with a garnish of black olives. This recipe will provide 4 such servings. Use the pâté to stuff celery too.

⚘ AVOCADO-STUFFED EGGS

SERVES 8 · 25 MINUTES

4 chilled hard-boiled eggs
1 lemon
1 ripe avocado pear
¼ teaspoon salt
Good pinch pepper

½ teaspoon prepared
  mustard
2 tablespoons mayonnaise
2 tablespoons chopped fresh
  chives or paprika
4 medium-sized tomatoes

88

DRESSING FOR TOMATOES

2 *tablespoons oil*	$\frac{1}{8}$ *teaspoon salt*
2 *teaspoons lemon juice*	2 *drops Tabasco*

8 *sprigs watercress*

1. Cut eggs into halves; remove yolks and put them through sieve. Save whites.
2. Squeeze lemon for juice. Keep lemon shells. Cut avocado pear in half and remove stone. Immediately rub halved lemon shells over halved avocado, squeezing shells for juice as you rub. Remove pulp from avocado pear. Mix with 1 tablespoon of lemon juice, and mash. Combine with sieved yolks, salt, pepper, mustard, and mayonnaise. Stuff whites with mixture, heaping it high. Chop chives, if you are using them, and slice tomatoes. Sprinkle eggs with chives or paprika. Eggs may be used as part of an hors d'oeuvres platter, or served on tomato slices with the following dressing.
3. Blend oil, lemon juice, salt, and Tabasco. Place tomato slices in attractive pattern on platter. Sprinkle with dressing. Set egg halves on tomato slices. Garnish with watercress.

✤ CHICKEN AND HAM PUFFS

SERVES 5 OR 6 · 25 TO 35 MINUTES

2 *cups fat or oil*	1 *tablespoon minced parsley*
1 *small onion*	2 *slices crustless white bread*
$\frac{1}{2}$ *tablespoon butter*	$\frac{1}{4}$ *cup milk*
1$\frac{1}{2}$ *cups ground cooked chicken*	3 *eggs, separated*
	Salt to taste
$\frac{2}{3}$ *cup minced ground cooked ham*	$\frac{1}{8}$ *teaspoon pepper*

1. Heat 2 cups of fat or oil in a deep fryer. Mince onion and sauté it in $\frac{1}{2}$ tablespoon of butter.

2. Prepare chicken, ham, onion, and parsley.

3. Mash bread in milk in a large bowl. Add onion with ground chicken, ham, and parsley, egg yolks, salt, and pepper.

4. Beat egg whites until stiff. Fold in.

5. Shape mixture into balls the size of walnuts and drop them, without crowding, into very hot fat. If they are difficult to shape, dip hands into cold water first. Fry balls until they are brown. Drain on paper towels. Serve hot.

As hors d'oeuvres, these may be served on toothpicks. Accompanied by SPANISH RICE, the light and tasty puffs make an excellent luncheon. ⟨

⟩₡ MEAT SALAD VINAIGRETTE

SERVES 6 TO 8 · PREPARATION 15 TO 20 MINUTES
CHILLING 2 TO 3 HOURS

1 *recipe* VINAIGRETTE SAUCE	¼ *cup cooked, smoked, or*
½ *clove garlic, crushed*	*corned tongue*
Dash of Tabasco	½ *cup boiled or roast fresh*
2 *cups cooked chicken, beef,*	*ham*
and veal in any combination	*Salt to taste*
	Lettuce

1 Prepare VINAIGRETTE SAUCE in a jar, adding garlic and Tabasco. Shake briskly.

2. Cut meats into short, thin strips. Shake sauce again and pour over meats. Mix thoroughly. Add salt if necessary. Chill 2 to 3 hours.

3. Serve on lettuce.

Fine for hors d'oeuvres platter, but omit lettuce.

✹ Suggested Hors d'Oeuvres Platter

MEAT SALAD VINAIGRETTE

CUCUMBER SALAD or CELERY-APPLE SALAD

WATERCRESS-POTATO SALAD or NIÇOISE SALAD

SARDINES or COLD SALMON, MAYONNAISE CAPER SAUCE

GARLIC BLACK OLIVES

Any 3 or more hors d'oeuvres will make a good platter provided there is variety in the choice of foods, for example, a fish dish, a meat dish, and a vegetable dish. Utilize leftover fish or meat; mince or cut julienne and add FRENCH DRESSING containing mustard, pickle, or capers to pep it up. Accompany the appetizers with French bread and butter or plain crackers.

✹ CARROTS À LA GRECQUE

SERVES 6 TO 8 · 25 MINUTES

6 *medium-sized carrots*	2 *peppercorns*
1 *cup water*	$\frac{1}{2}$ *small bay leaf*
1 *tablespoon olive oil*	*Pinch thyme*
3 *tablespoons salad oil*	*Pinch coriander*
$\frac{1}{4}$ *cup lemon juice*	6 *or* 8 *fennel seeds*
$\frac{1}{2}$ *teaspoon salt*	

1. Scrape carrots and cut them into sticks, about 4 inches long by $\frac{3}{8}$ of an inch thick.
2. Add to water the oils, lemon juice, seasoning, and spices. Bring to a boil. Add carrots and cook over medium heat 8 to 10 minutes or until carrots are almost tender.
3. Transfer carrots in slotted spoon to a dish. Strain hot carrot liquid over sticks. Refrigerate when cool.
4. Serve chilled in an hors-d'oeuvres dish with just the liquor that clings to sticks.

Carrots prepared thus may also be used for salad. They are a fine change from raw carrots. Use them, too, in an antipasto plate along with ITALIAN TOMATO SALAD, FENNEL STICKS, Italian salami, capocolla, or prosciutto, sliced thinly, and Italian tinned tuna. The sliced cold meats can be purchased at almost any delicatessen. Buy tuna labelled "tonno" and serve as it comes from the tin with its oil. Pass a plate of thickly sliced Italian or French bread and butter, or lightly toasted and buttered sliced hard rolls. Unsalted or slightly salted bread sticks will do too.

MARINATED MUSHROOMS ·

SERVES 6 TO 8 · PREPARATION 15 MINUTES
REFRIGERATION 24 HOURS

½ *pound small mushrooms*	½ *teaspoon salt*
1 *clove garlic*	6 *fennel seeds*
1 *cup water*	2 *peppercorns*
1 *tablespoon olive oil*	½ *small bay leaf*
3 *tablespoons salad oil*	*Pinch coriander*
5 *tablespoons mild white*	*Pinch thyme*
vinegar, preferably wine	
vinegar	

1. Cut off thin slices from ends of mushroom stems and discard. Wipe mushrooms with damp cloth. Split garlic into halves.
2. Combine all ingredients except mushrooms and bring to boil. Add mushrooms and cook briskly 5 minutes.
3. Remove mushrooms. Strain liquid over them and refrigerate when cool in a covered jar or dish.
4. Use after 24 hours. Serve impaled on toothpicks.

These mushrooms are mild, with a slightly tart taste. For a stronger flavour, keep in the marinade 3 or 4 days.

❧ GARLIC BLACK OLIVES

PREPARATION 5 MINUTES
PREPARE AT LEAST 2 DAYS AHEAD

1 *medium-sized tin* *mammoth-size black olives*	5 or 6 *cloves garlic*

1. At least 2 days before they are to be served, empty olives and liquid into a jar. Spear peeled garlic cloves with toothpick and drop into jar. Cover jar and shake it well before storing in refrigerator. Shake occasionally from time to time to spread garlic flavour.
2. Remove garlic when olives are seasoned to your taste.
3. Serve with antipasto, on a RAW VEGETABLE PLATTER, or with salad.

These may be kept around for 2 or 3 weeks at least. I sometimes don't even bother to remove the garlic.

❧ RAW VEGETABLE PLATTER

Young carrots	*Cucumbers, medium-sized*
1 *teaspoon sugar for each* ½ *cup water*	*and firm*
Pascal celery, leafy part	*Red radishes, firm and*
removed	*without cracks*
Green peppers, large,	*Cherry or plum tomatoes*
fleshy, and firm	GARLIC BLACK OLIVES
Fennel, medium-sized	SOUR CREAM DUNK SAUCE

93

1. CARROT STICKS: Peel carrots. Cut into even strips, about ¾ inch wide and 4 inches long. Place in cold water; add sugar and refrigerate.

2. CELERY STICKS: Follow above procedure, but omit sugar.

3. GREEN PEPPER STICKS: Same as for celery sticks.

4. FENNEL STICKS: Same as for celery sticks.

5. CUCUMBER STICKS: Cut cucumber into 4 parts lengthwise. Then cut each quarter crosswise in half. Scoop out seeds. Cut each section into strips. Place in cold water in refrigerator until ready to be used.

6. CARROT CURLS: Choose carrots of uniform size. Trim off short piece from narrow end. With potato peeler, cut paper-thin slices lengthwise. Roll each into ring and fasten with toothpick to help keep shape. Refrigerate in cold water several hours. Remove toothpick.

7. CELERY CURLS: Remove leaves. Cut each rib into 3-inch sections. Cut fringelike strips at both ends almost to centre of each section. Store in ice water in refrigerator several hours until ends curl up.

8. RED RADISHES: Leave a bit of the stem. Crisp in ice water for several hours.

9. RADISH ROSES: Cut off the root taper. Begin at root end and with a sharp knife cut thin strips of red peel about ⅜ inch to ½ inch wide almost to the stem end. Crisp in ice water several hours. Petals will open up.

10. CHERRY OR PLUM TOMATOES: Simply chill. If they are home-grown and freshly picked, serve without chilling as they are especially delicious this way.

Drain vegetables. Arrange them in groups on a round platter with a bowl of sauce in the centre. Select those that you like, of course, but try to include tomatoes or radishes or both for texture and colour, and olives for a tasty accent. See FRENCH MAYONNAISE, for an extra sauce.

⅍ SOUR CREAM DUNK SAUCE

MAKES 1¼ CUPS · PREPARATION 5 MINUTES
CHILLING AT LEAST 3 HOURS

1 *cup sour cream*	¼ *teaspoon salt*
1 *tablespoon tomato paste*	⅛ *teaspoon white pepper*
¼ *cup bland oil*	⅛ *teaspoon sugar*
2 *tablespoons wine vinegar*	½ *clove garlic, crushed*
2 *tablespoons chopped fresh*	
dill	

1. Combine sour cream and tomato paste in a pint jar.

2. Add all other ingredients. Shake vigorously.

3. Chill several hours or overnight.

Use also as a dip for shrimp, and as a dressing for crab meat
and cucumber salads.

⅍ SUMMER VEGETABLE RELISH BOWL

Celery sticks	*Radish roses*
Carrot sticks	*Garlic black olives*
Cucumber sticks	*Green olives*
Fennel sticks	*Bowl of crushed ice*

1. Prepare vegetables according to directions in RAW VEGETABLE
PLATTER and GARLIC BLACK OLIVES.

2. Store vegetables separately in ice water.

3. When ready to serve, tuck vegetable sticks into crushed ice in
well-spaced pattern. Scatter radishes and olives over ice.

SOME CHOICE SOUPS

❌   ❌   ❌   ❌   ❌   ❌   ❌   ❌

OUP-MAKING can take a lot of time. To keep a stock pot
simmering for hours is impractical, if not impossible, in
the modern small kitchen. The soups in this section have,
therefore, been chosen for the ease with which they can be
made. In the recipes given here, tinned broth or consommé
may substitute for fresh stock. Where leeks are specified, you
may substitute celery or onion when they are not available,
except in the recipes for leek and potato soup and Vichyssoise,
in which leeks are essential. Serve hot soups hot and chilled ones
very cold.

Flour, potato, and rice may be used to thicken soups: flour to
thicken any soup, potato or rice where their flavour is suitable.
The procedure for the use of these thickeners is this: Sauté
minced vegetables slowly, without browning, in butter (1 pound
of vegetables to 2 or 3 tablespoons of butter) for 15 to 20
minutes. Sauté small leafy vegetables briefly, only until wilted.
Do not sauté asparagus or cauliflower. Blend in 2 tablespoons of
flour or add 2 medium-sized minced raw potatoes or 4 tablespoons of raw rice. Add 2 cups of hot light consommé and
seasoning, and cook until the vegetables are very soft. Press all
through food mill, or cool and turn into blender. Finish soup

by diluting it with milk, cream, or more stock to the consistency you prefer, and reheat. Just before serving, add 1 teaspoon to 1 tablespoon butter. Soup that is made with stock as the liquid and flour as the thickener may be improved by the addition of 1 or 2 raw egg yolks mixed with 2 or 3 tablespoons of cream away from the heat.

Asparagus and cauliflower require special treatment. If flour is the thickener, blend it with hot butter, stir in the consommé, and bring it to a boil. Then add the minced vegetables raw, season, and proceed as directed. If using potato to thicken a cauliflower soup, both vegetables should be minced and added raw to the hot stock. Thickening agents and some soups they go with follow:

FLOUR: watercress, spinach, chives, lettuce, Belgian endive, chicory, celery, cucumber, cauliflower, asparagus, pumpkin
POTATO: turnip, pumpkin, broccoli, celery, Brussels sprouts, carrot, cauliflower
RICE: carrot, turnip, pumpkin

⅍ CHILLED BORSCHT

SERVES 5 OR 6 · PREPARATION 1¼ HOURS
CHILLING 3 HOURS

1 *bunch beets (about 5)*	1½ *teaspoons salt*
1 *medium onion*	¾ *teaspoon sour salt*
1 *medium apple*	1 *teaspoon sugar*
1½ *cups shredded cabbage*	¾ *cup sour cream*
5 *cups cold water*	

1. Cut off leafy parts of beets without cutting into beets. Scrub unpeeled beets. Coarsely grate them into a pot. Mince onion and unpeeled apple. Shred cabbage. Add to beets.

2. Add water and salt. Bring to a boil; then cook slowly 1 hour.

3. Strain soup into another saucepan, pressing beets with spoon to extract all juice. Discard solid beet mixture. Return soup to

97

heat. Add sour salt and sugar. Taste. Borscht should be sourish with a suggestion of slight winy sweetness.

4. Chill soup until very cold. If you have glass bowls, use these for serving. Float 1 or 2 tablespoons sour cream in each bowl.

For best results, this soup should really be chilled overnight. Chilled borscht is sometimes served with small, boiled potatoes. The contrast in temperatures is excellent.

✖ HOT BORSCHT

SERVES 4 · 1½ TO 1¾ HOURS

1 *bunch beets (about 5)*	1 *tablespoon lemon juice or*
2 *tablespoons butter*	*more to taste*
1 *cup hot water*	2 *teaspoons sugar*
3½ *cups hot veal or chicken*	2 *eggs, beaten*
stock	½ *cup sour cream*

1. Cut off leafy parts of beets except for 2 inches of stem. Snip off these stems without cutting into beet. Rinse stem pieces and save. Scrub unpeeled beets. Peel off about ½ inch of rough skin at stem end. Shred beets.

2. Melt butter in a saucepan; when it is hot, add beets and cook slowly 15 to 20 minutes. Add ¼ cup hot water, stir and cook slowly until water is absorbed. Add remaining hot water, ¼ cup at a time, and repeat process until beets are almost tender, about ½ hour.

3. Add stock and stems; bring to a boil. Cook slowly 30 minutes or until beets are very tender. Strain soup into another pan; discard shredded beets and stems. Add lemon juice and sugar. Stir and taste. The soup should have a rich winy taste, more sour than sweet. It may need a pinch of salt. Add more lemon juice and sugar if it needs them, but do it cautiously. Turn off heat.

4. Beat eggs a few seconds. Add 4 tablespoons beet liquid slowly. Return mixture to soup gradually, stirring. Do not boil soup after this.

5. Serve soup hot. Top with 1 or 2 tablespoons sour cream per bowl of soup.

Leftover soup may be served well chilled, but be sure to remove any fat that has congealed on surface.

⚜ CABBAGE SOUP

SERVES 6 · 35 MINUTES

1 *large onion*	*Salt to taste*
2½ *tablespoons butter*	⅛ *teaspoon freshly ground*
1 *small white turnip*	*black pepper*
1 *small white cabbage, about*	*Pinch thyme*
1 *pound*	½ *cup sour cream (optional)*
4 *cups hot stock, beef and*	
chicken in any proportion	

1. Mince onion finely. Melt 1½ tablespoons of butter in a saucepan; add onion when butter is hot and cook slowly 10 minutes without browning.

2. Cut turnip and cabbage into short thin shreds. Put 1 tablespoon of butter in saucepan. When butter has melted add turnip and cabbage. Toss them in butter 2 or 3 minutes.

3. Cover with hot stock. Season with salt to taste, pepper, and thyme. Bring to a boil; cook slowly 15 minutes.

4. Serve soup hot. Top each serving with 1 tablespoon of sour cream if desired.

This quickly-made soup is very good if cabbage is not permitted to overcook.

✕ CREAM OF CARROT SOUP

SERVES 5 OR 6 · 45 MINUTES

1 *large onion*	1¼ *cups hot veal or chicken*
3 *large carrots*	*stock*
2 *to* 3 *tablespoons butter*	2 *cups warm milk*
Pinch salt	*Pinch nutmeg*
¼ *teaspoon sugar*	*Salt to taste*
1 *large potato*	⅛ *teaspoon white pepper*
1½ *tablespoons flour*	1 *tablespoon chopped chives*
	or parsley

1. Mince onion. Grate carrots coarsely. Melt butter in a saucepan; add onion, carrots, salt, and sugar. Cook slowly 10 minutes. Slice potato.

2. With a wire whisk stir in flour until it is absorbed. Add stock, stirring constantly, and bring to a boil. Add potato slices. Cook gently until vegetables are soft enough to strain, about 20 minutes.

3. Add milk, nutmeg, salt to taste, and pepper. Bring to a boil and strain or press through food mill. Reheat without boiling. Chop chives or parsley.

4. Sprinkle soup with chives or parsley and serve hot.

If you would like a richer soup, substitute light or medium cream for half the milk. Add the cup of milk as directed above, but do not stir in cream until after soup has been strained. Do not boil.

✕ SOUP ST. GERMAIN · Purée of Fresh Green Peas

SERVES 4 · 45 MINUTES

1½ *pounds fresh green peas*	3 *lettuce leaves*
1 *leek, green part only, or* 1	3 *tablespoons butter*
small rib celery	⅓ *cup water*

100

$\frac{1}{4}$ *teaspoon salt*
$\frac{1}{8}$ *teaspoon sugar*
Pinch dried chervil

2 cups hot chicken stock
$\frac{1}{4}$ *cup light cream*

1. Shell peas, slice leek or celery, and shred lettuce. In a pot, cook vegetables slowly in butter, water, and seasonings until they are soft. Reserve 2 tablespoons of whole cooked peas.
2. Mash vegetables in the pot. Add hot stock and bring to a boil. Pour soup through a food mill or sieve into another pot, and press mashed vegetables through. Add reserved peas and cream; reheat soup but do not allow to boil.
3. To keep soup hot without boiling it, place it over hot water.
4. Serve soup hot with a few peas in each plate.

✂ ONION SOUP

SERVES 5 OR 6 · 50 MINUTES

4 large onions
3 to 4 tablespoons butter
1 teaspoon flour
1 clove garlic, crushed
Good pinch dry mustard
3 cups beef consommé
$\frac{3}{4}$ *cup water*

$\frac{1}{4}$ *cup dry white wine*
Salt to taste
$\frac{1}{8}$ *teaspoon pepper*
1 cup grated Parmesan cheese
5 or 6 slices French bread or
   hard roll

1. Slice onions thinly. Cut slices in half and shake shreds apart.

2. Melt butter in a heavy pot over low heat. Add onions when butter is hot and cook until brown, about 20 minutes.

3. Blend flour, crushed garlic, and mustard into onions until smooth. Add consommé, water, wine, salt, and pepper; stir and bring to a boil. Cover and cook slowly 15 minutes. Add 2 tablespoons of grated cheese and cook 5 minutes.

4. Toast bread lightly. Fill bowls with soup. Float slice of toast in each; sprinkle bread with about 1 tablespoon of cheese.

5. Serve hot with remaining cheese.

✄ MINESTRONE

SERVES 6 · SOAKING OVERNIGHT
PREPARATION 3 TO 3¾ HOURS
WITH PRE-COOKED BEANS 55 MINUTES

1 *cup dried pea beans or chick peas*	3 *sprigs parsley*
¼ *pound salt pork*	2 *tablespoons oil*
6 *cups cold water*	4 *tablespoons tomato paste*
2 *ribs celery*	*Salt to taste*
1 *cup shredded cabbage*	¼ *teaspoon pepper*
1 *large carrot*	3 *tablespoons green peas*
1 *medium-sized potato*	¼ *cup raw rice*
1 *clove garlic*	*Good pinch basil*
1 *small onion*	½ *cup grated Parmesan cheese*

1. Soak beans or chick peas overnight in cold water to cover. Drain.
2. Cube salt pork; add with drained beans or peas to water. Bring slowly to a boil and simmer legumes covered until tender, anywhere from 2 to 3 hours.
3. Slice celery thinly. Shred cabbage finely. Cube carrot and potato. Add vegetables to beans. Mince garlic, onion, and parsley. Cook in hot oil until onion is soft but not brown. Add to soup with tomato paste, salt to taste, and pepper. Cook slowly 20 minutes.
4. Add green peas and rice. Cook 20 minutes. Powder basil with fingers and sprinkle over soup.
5. Serve hot with bowl of grated cheese.

If more liquid is needed, add water that is boiling. Use freshly grated cheese if it is available. Dried beans and peas vary greatly in cooking time. To save time, the soaked beans may be cooked the day before (see Step 2) and refrigerated. They may also be cooked quickly, unsoaked, in a pressure cooker.

❧ POTATO AND LEEK SOUP

SERVES 4 TO 5 · 45 MINUTES

4 *large leeks, white part only*	2 *cups chicken broth*
1 *large onion*	*Salt to taste*
2 *tablespoons butter*	⅛ *teaspoon white pepper*
4 *large potatoes*	1 *cup milk*
1 *rib celery*	1 *teaspoon butter*

1. Cut leeks in half lengthwise. Wash them well to remove grit. Then cut them crosswise into thin slices. Mince onion.

2. Sauté these in hot butter in a saucepan over low heat 15 minutes, without browning.

3. Slice potatoes and celery thinly. Add these to broth with leeks and onions, seasoning them with salt and pepper. Bring to a boil. Cook vegetables slowly, covered, until they are tender enough to mash. Add milk and heat without boiling.

4. Put soup with vegetables through a food mill or press them through a sieve. Or cool and put them through an electric blender until mixture is smooth. Reheat soup without boiling. Add butter in small bits, stirring. Serve hot.

If soup is too thick, dilute it with a little hot milk. Use of blender saves 5 to 10 minutes' time.

❧ Variation I · VICHYSSOISE

SERVES 4 TO 6 · PREPARATION 30 MINUTES
CHILLING OVERNIGHT

1. Follow Step 1.

2. Omit Step 2. Follow Step 3, using onion but omitting milk.

3. Follow Step 4. Instead of reheating, stir soup and chill it until it is icy cold.

4. Just before serving, mix in 1½ to 2 cups light or medium cream. Sprinkle each serving with 1 teaspoon finely chopped fresh chives. Serve cold.

A less rich Vichyssoise may be made by adding half milk and half medium cream. There is no substitute for chives in this dish. Nothing else flavours it so subtly.

✴ Variation II · POTATO AND WATERCRESS SOUP

SERVES 6 · 35 MINUTES

Eliminate leeks and celery.

1. Follow Steps 1 and 2, cooking onion only 5 minutes. Then add 1 bunch watercress and sauté until it is wilted, about 2 or 3 minutes.
2. Follow Step 3. Add onion and watercress along with an extra cup of milk.
3. Follow Step 4, adding pinch of nutmeg and allspice before reheating soup.

✴ EGG DROP SOUP

SERVES 5 OR 6 · 5 MINUTES

1 *quart chicken broth*	*Pinch salt*
3 *eggs*	*Pinch pepper*
1½ *tablespoons flour*	2 *tablespoons chopped parsley*
2 *tablespoons grated*	
Parmesan cheese	

1. Have ready boiling chicken broth.
2. Beat eggs until thick. Mix in flour, cheese, salt, and pepper; beat thoroughly until these ingredients are well combined.
3. Drizzle egg mixture slowly into boiling soup; stir constantly

and vigorously with a wire whisk. Reduce heat immediately and simmer 5 minutes. Remove soup from heat. Chop parsley.

4. When ready to serve soup, whisk it up again; pour into cups or tureen. Sprinkle with parsley.

This may be made just with eggs, without flour and cheese. After eggs are added, no additional simmering is needed. An excellent way to serve eggs to one who cannot tolerate an egg that tastes like an egg.

⅍ CONSOMMÉ CELESTINE

SERVES 5 OR 6 · 10 MINUTES

1 *quart hot chicken consommé, fresh or tinned*	½ *recipe pancakes for* CHEESE BLINTZES

1. Make pancakes as in recipe for CHEESE BLINTZES. You will need about 3 for use here.
2. Roll each pancake neatly. With a sharp knife, cut rolls crosswise into fine shreds. Shake them out.
3. Add pancake shreds to hot soup and serve.

⅍ CHICKEN GUMBO SOUP

SERVES 6 TO 8 · 1¼ HOURS

¼-*pound slice raw ham*	*Few grains cayenne*
2 *quarters of fryer, any parts*	*Good pinch thyme*
3 *tablespoons butter or lard*	1 *bay leaf*
1 *medium-sized onion*	3 *tomatoes*
6 *cups boiling water*	½ *pound fresh okra or* 10
3 *chicken bouillon cubes*	*ounces frozen okra*
¼ *teaspoon pepper*	2 *tablespoons raw rice*

1. Dice ham. Skin, bone, and dice 1 chicken part. Save skin and bones.

2. Melt butter or lard in a large saucepan or soup pot. When it is hot, add ham, diced chicken, and whole chicken part; brown well. Mince onion and add towards end of browning process to brown slightly. Stir frequently.

3. Add water, bouillon cubes, pepper, cayenne, thyme, bay leaf, and reserved skin and bones. Bring to a boil; then cover and cook slowly 30 minutes.

4. Peel, seed, and mince tomatoes, and add them to soup. Add okra, fresh or frozen, and rice. Bring soup back to boil and cook slowly about 30 minutes.

5. Remove bay leaf, skin, bones, and chicken part. Serve soup in deep bowls. If you wish, mince whole chicken part and add some to each serving.

This thick soup is good as a main course for lunch.

A VARIETY OF VEGETABLES

✕ ✕ ✕ ✕ ✕ ✕ ✕ ✕

VEGETABLES are mistreated more often than any other food. When they are cooked in too much liquid or too long, they lose not only their natural good flavour but their health-supporting vitamins as well. They are delicious when steamed or cooked until just tender in very little boiling water or broth, slightly salted or unsalted. A bit of butter added, a tossing together with a sprinkling of salt, pepper, and whatever other seasoning pleases you, and voilà! To be more exact, add either 1 chicken bouillon cube or ½ teaspoon of salt to each cup of water used; bring it to a boil, and throw in prepared vegetables. Use only enough liquid so that almost all of it has evaporated by the time the vegetables are tender. This requires watching, however, towards the end of the cooking time. Then stir in 1 tablespoon of butter, cut into bits, for every 4 servings; season, and toss over low heat 5 to 10 seconds. Dust with finely-chopped parsley, chives, mint, or any other fresh herb that suits the vegetable and you have a truly delicious thing. Try this treatment with frozen vegetables too. Just remember these rules:

1. Cook in very little boiling liquid.
2. Cook until just tender.

3. Keep green vegetables green by cooking them rapidly, covered, 5 to 8 minutes. Then uncover partially and complete cooking.

Almost all vegetables may be prepared beforehand and refrigerated or stored in a cool place, or in cold water. Even though there is a reported vitamin loss for many vegetables when this is done, the advantage of early preparation is important to practically all cooks.

ASPARAGUS: Break off end of stalk where it snaps easily, a little above where the light part merges into the green. Remove scales, wash very well, drain, and store in crisper.

AUBERGINE: Do not peel until just before cooking. Keep in cool place.

GREEN BEANS: Wash quickly in cold water. Nip off ends. Store in covered container in refrigerator.

BEETS: Cut off all but 2 inches of tops. If beets are young, save tops and cook like spinach from 5 to 15 minutes. Scrub beets well. Let drain. Store in paper-lined refrigerator dish to prevent discoloration of dish.

BROCCOLI: Cut off tough ends of stems. Remove leaves. If stems are more than ¾ inch thick, make several lengthwise gashes from bottom of stem almost to flowerlets. Place in salted, cold water 10 minutes to draw out sand, insects, etc. Lift out, rinse, and let drain. Refrigerate in covered dish.

CABBAGE: Cut in half and rinse in cold water. Drain. Cut into wedges and core. Or cut into quarters, core, remove thick ribs, and shred. Place in crisper.

CARROTS: Trim both ends. Scrape or pare with potato peeler. Store in cold water, cut up or whole.

CAULIFLOWER: Remove all green stalks. Soak in cold, salted water 10 minutes. Lift out, rinse, and drain. Separate into flowerlets if desired. Store in refrigerator dish.

CELERY: Cut off leafy parts. Trim roots. Separate into ribs and wash thoroughly. Let drain. Place in covered refrigerator tray or stand in cold water.

CUCUMBER: Do not pare or cut until ready to cook. Cover and refrigerate.

ENDIVE, ESCAROLE, CHICORY:

Endive: Blanched with leaves tightly folded, forming a slender, elongated stalk; often called Belgian endive. It is best to wash and separate into leaves a few minutes before using.

Curly endive or Chicory: Sometimes called French endive. Salad green with tightly curled, long narrow leaves, dark green on the outside and light near the centre. Lighter parts are more tender and delicately bitter. Rinse under cold water. drain, and let dry. Place in crisper. Cut into bite-size pieces at last minute. Discard tough parts.

Escarole: Broad-leaved, flat, and spreading, with light centres. Rinse, drain, and store covered in refrigerator.

FENNEL: Scrape bulb, cut off leafy part, rinse, and drain. For salad, cut bulb in thin slices crosswise. To eat like celery, cut lengthwise in quarters or sixths right through bulb and stalk. For cooking, slice across in 1-inch sections. Store in refrigerator, covered and whole. Save leaves to use where anise flavour is desirable.

LEEKS: Cut off 2 inches of green tops unless otherwise directed. Wash well in cold water to remove interior grit. Cover and store in refrigerator.

MUSHROOMS: Keep whole and dry until ready to cook. Avoid washing if possible. Wipe with damp cloth or rub with cut lemon. Stems, if solid and tender, may be left attached to caps. It is not necessary to peel mushrooms.

OKRA: Choose young tender pods that snap easily. Wash and drain. Cut off stem end. Use whole or sliced. Store whole in covered refrigerator dish.

PARSNIPS: Scrape or peel. For use as vegetable course, leave whole if small; cube or slice if large. For soup greens, leave whole or halve. Store whole or cut up in covered refrigerator dish.

PEAS: Try to shell just before cooking. If not convenient, shell and refrigerate unwashed in covered dish. Rinse before cooking.

SPINACH: Tear off root ends and thick stems. Place in large quantity of cold water and lift out so any grit at bottom of dish is not stirred up. Repeat 4 or 5 times. Let drain. Place loosely in covered refrigerator container.

SUMMER SQUASH (YELLOW): Wash well and dry. Cut off small piece at each end. Store whole and unpeeled in refrigerator dish. Do not peel even for cooking.

TOMATOES: Store ripe ones unwashed in refrigerator. To ripen semi-ripe tomatoes, place them in a small paper bag; close bag and keep at room temperature away from direct sunlight 2 to 4 days, depending upon degree of ripeness.

TURNIPS (WHITE): Remove green tops. Tops of young turnips may be cooked like spinach from 15 to 25 minutes. Scrub roots and dry. Store in cool place. Peel just before cooking; leave whole, slice, or cube.

WATERCRESS: Pick over leaves; remove wilted and bruised ones. Rinse, drain, and let dry. Store in crisper. Snip or tear into pieces just before using.

ZUCCHINI [BABY MARROWS]: Wash and let drain. Cut off stem and blossom ends. Store whole in crisper. Cook unpeeled.

⅜ ARTICHOKES, RUSSIAN DRESSING

SERVES 6 · 40 TO 55 MINUTES

6 *small artichokes*	1 *slice lemon*
1 *clove garlic*	*Salted water almost to cover*

RUSSIAN DRESSING

½ *cup mayonnaise*	1 *tablespoon oil*
1 *tablespoon ketchup*	2 *teaspoons vinegar*

110

1. Soak artichokes in salted cold water 15 minutes. Rinse off. Remove 3 or 4 outer tough leaves. Cut off two-thirds of stem. With sharp knife cut off about ⅜ inch of tops of artichokes to remove prickly tips of leaves.

2. Add garlic and lemon slice to salted water and bring to boil. Drop in artichokes, cover and cook over medium heat from 20 to 35 minutes depending upon size. When fork pierces stem easily, remove from pan and drain.

3. To make RUSSIAN DRESSING, combine mayonnaise, ketchup, oil, and vinegar in small bowl. Use as a dunk sauce. Pull off leaves one by one, and dunk tender tips into sauce. Cut off fuzzy inedible part or choke and discard. Eat remaining edible portion with sauce.

This vegetable requires all one's attention when eaten. Serve it also separately as a first course.

⅍ ASPARAGUS WITH BUTTERED CRUMBS

SERVES 4 TO 6 · 35 MINUTES

2 *pounds asparagus stalks*	¼ *teaspoon lemon juice*
Boiling, salted water	3 *tablespoons butter*
to barely cover	
2 *tablespoons fresh fine bread-*	
crumbs	

1. Prepare asparagus. Have ready boiling, salted water.

2. Cook asparagus uncovered and rapidly until it is tender, about 15 minutes. Drain it well. Keep it warm.

3. Prepare breadcrumbs. Have ready lemon juice.

4. Just before serving, brown crumbs in 2 tablespoons butter 1 minute. Add and melt other tablespoon of butter without browning. Remove from heat. Add lemon juice. Dress asparagus tips with mixture.

111

❧ Variation · ASPARAGUS FLAMANDE

SERVES 4 TO 6 · 40 TO 45 MINUTES

1. Have ready 2 sieved hard-boiled egg yolks and 1½ tablespoons chopped parsley.
2. Follow Steps 1 and 2 above. Omit Steps 3 and 4.
3. Just before serving, melt 4 tablespoons butter in a small pan without permitting it to brown. Remove it from heat and immediately mix in sieved yolks, a good pinch of salt, and freshly ground black pepper. Pour over asparagus and serve, sprinkled with parsley. ⟍

The egg sauce may be prepared ahead and refrigerated. When it is needed, reheat it a few seconds, just long enough to melt butter.

❧ GREEN BEANS AMANDINE

SERVES 4 OR 5 · 30 MINUTES

1 *pound green beans or 1*	1 *tablespoon butter*
packet frozen beans,	¼ *cup blanched almonds*
French-style	2 *tablespoons butter*
1 *small onion*	⅛ *teaspoon freshly ground*
1¼ *cups boiling salted water*	*black pepper*

1. Cut fresh beans into slivers. Peel onion. Cook fresh beans with onion in 1¼ cups boiling, salted water or cook frozen beans in ⅔ cup boiling, salted water. Let boil rapidly 5 minutes. Uncover them to preserve colour and cook them over moderate heat until they are tender but firm, about 15 to 20 minutes more. Pour off liquid if any is left. Remove onion.
2. Shake pan over low heat to allow moisture to evaporate. Add 1 tablespoon butter, cut into small bits, shaking pan to distribute it. Season beans with more salt if necessary.

112

3. While beans cook, shred almonds and sauté them in 2 tablespoons of hot butter until they are light brown. Toss over drained beans and mix. Sprinkle beans with pepper and serve hot.

✖ KIDNEY BEANS, MEXICAN STYLE

SERVES 6 TO 8 · 2 TO 2½ HOURS

1 *pound (2 cups) dried kidney beans*	2 *tablespoons bacon fat or butter*
6 *cups cold water*	1–2 *teaspoons chili powder*
1 *small onion, stick with 2 cloves*	¼ *teaspoon salt*
1 *whole carrot*	1 *small tin tomato sauce (6 ounces)*
1 *bay leaf*	½ *teaspoon oregano*
2 *teaspoons salt*	1 *medium-sized Bermuda onion*
¼ *teaspoon pepper*	
1 *large onion*	½ *cup grated Cheddar cheese*

1. Wash beans. Soak in water overnight.
2. Do not drain beans. Add small onion, carrot, bay leaf, salt, and pepper. Bring to boil slowly and simmer 1½ to 2 hours or until beans are tender. Drain, reserving 1 cup liquid. Discard onion, carrot, and bay leaf.
3. Slice large onion thinly. Melt bacon fat or butter in a frying-pan. Cook onion slowly 5 minutes. Sprinkle over it 1 teaspoon chili powder and ¼ teaspoon salt. Stir and cook 1 minute. Add tomato sauce, bean broth, and oregano. Bring to boil.
3. Add tomato sauce mixture to drained beans in pot. Stir to mix well. Taste. Add extra chili powder and salt if necessary. Cook slowly 10 minutes to blend flavours.
5. Mince Bermuda onion. Grate cheese. Pass each separately to sprinkle over beans.

This dish may be cooked the day before it is needed; it improves upon reheating. Leftover cooked pork, beef, and lamb may be combined with the cooked beans and reheated together for a very palatable dish. If beans are too dry, use additional tomato sauce and pep up with more chili powder if desired.

❧ BROCCOLI SAUTÉ

SERVES 4 TO 6 · 40 MINUTES

1 *bunch fresh broccoli*	2 *garlic cloves*
Unsalted boiling water	$\frac{1}{2}$ *teaspoon salt*
barely to cover	$\frac{1}{8}$ *teaspoon freshly ground*
2 *tablespoons olive oil*	*black pepper*

1. Prepare broccoli for cooking.
2. Arrange stalks 1 layer thick in a large skillet. Add boiling water. Cover and boil over medium-low heat 8 minutes. Partially uncover to keep green colour and cook until tender but quite firm, about 7 to 10 minutes. Drain thoroughly.
3. Heat oil in a dry skillet. Mince garlic and sauté until light brown. Add broccoli, seasoning with salt. Cook 5 or 6 minutes, uncovered, gently turning and stirring. Season with pepper and serve hot.

Frozen broccoli may be used. Cook according to directions but without adding salt to cooking water. Follow Steps 2 and 3.

❧ Variation I · BROCCOLI, HOLLANDAISE SAUCE

SERVES 4 TO 6 · 35 MINUTES

1. Follow Steps 1 and 2. Keep vegetable warm.
2. Make sauce while broccoli cooks or, if you prefer, beforehand.
3. Arrange well-drained broccoli on a platter. Distribute sauce over broccoli, or serve it separately in a sauceboat. Double recipe if more sauce is desired.

✄ HOLLANDAISE SAUCE

MAKES ABOUT ½ CUP · 8 TO 10 MINUTES

4 *tablespoons butter*	2 *tablespoons cold water*
2 *egg yolks*	⅛ *teaspoon salt*
1 *tablespoon lemon juice*	*Few grains cayenne*

1. Pour about an inch of water into bottom of a double boiler and bring to boil. Lower heat. Set top part of boiler over it, making sure water does not touch bottom of pot.

2. Melt 2 tablespoons butter in top part. Add unbeaten egg yolks, lemon juice, water, salt, and cayenne. With wire whisk, keep stirring until sauce is smooth and begins to thicken, usually less than 1 minute. (If eggs threaten to curdle, that is, if any white specks appear, lift out pan from hot water immediately, as it has cooked either too long or is too hot.) With top out of hot water, away from heat, stir in remaining 2 tablespoonfuls of butter, and whisk until it is melted.

3. Try to use sauce at once, but if this is not possible, place sauce over an inch or two of tepid water and cover. Or refrigerate and when ready to use, heat over tepid water, away from burner.

There is nothing mysterious about making this sauce. It's simple and speedy to do. Just be sure to keep heat very low to prevent curdling. An equal amount of orange juice, tarragon vinegar, or sherry may replace lemon juice if flavour is suitable. Use with poached or steamed fish, hot fish mousse, and other vegetables like cauliflower and asparagus.

✄ Variation II · HOT BROCCOLI SALAD

SERVES 4 TO 6 · 30 MINUTES

1. Follow Steps 1 and 2. Omit Step 3.

2. Combine in small jar: 3 tablespoons olive oil, 2 tablespoons lemon juice, 1 small clove crushed garlic, ¼ teaspoon salt,

⅛ teaspoon freshly ground black pepper, and 1 tablespoon chopped parsley. Shake well.

3. Pour dressing evenly over broccoli, and serve.

✂ STEAMED CHOPPED BROCCOLI

SERVES 4 · 25 MINUTES

1 *packet frozen chopped broccoli*	*Few drops lemon juice (optional)*
1½ *cups water*	– 1 *tablespoon butter, melted*
1 *chicken bouillon cube*	*(optional)*
Freshly ground black pepper	

1. Drop bouillon cube into a pot with water, and bring to boiling point. Stir until bouillon cube is dissolved. Place rack or trivet in pot. Lay frozen broccoli block on rack. Cover tightly and let steam over medium-high heat about 10 minutes. Vegetables should be thawed by this time. Stir to break up any lumps. Cover and continue to steam for 10 minutes. There should be a few tablespoonfuls of liquid left. Broccoli should be tender.

2. Combine liquid with broccoli and stir well; liquid may be salty. Serve with a sprinkling of pepper, or squeeze a few drops of lemon juice over broccoli and season with pepper. If you wish to use the butter, use only 1 tablespoon of pan liquid. Pour butter over vegetable. Turn them gently and coat. Season if necessary.

✂ BRUSSELS SPROUTS SAUTÉ

SERVES 6 · 40 MINUTES

2 *cups Brussels sprouts*	1 *garlic clove (optional)*
1 *chicken bouillon cube*	2 *tablespoons butter*
1 *cup water*	*Salt to taste*
1 *tablespoon parsley*	⅛ *teaspoon pepper*

1. Strip off outer discoloured leaves of sprouts. Cut off stems. Soak in cold salted water 15 minutes to draw out sand, etc. Lift out of water and rinse.

2. Add bouillon cube to water and bring to boil. Drop in Brussels sprouts; bring back to boil and cook uncovered over medium-low heat 10 to 15 minutes until sprouts are tender. Drain. Slice. Chop parsley. Mince garlic.

3. Heat butter in pan slowly. Add garlic and cook in butter 2 or 3 minutes. Add sprouts; toss them in butter until they are lightly browned. Correct seasoning. Sprinkle with parsley.

4. Serve hot.

Leftover cold Brussels sprouts may be revived by sautéing them this way.

⅍ BRAISED RED CABBAGE

SERVES 4 · 1 HOUR

1 *pound red cabbage* *washed, well drained*	1 *tablespoon water*
	2 *teaspoons wine vinegar*
1 *small onion*	1 *tablespoon brown sugar*
1 *tart apple*	½ *teaspoon salt*
2 *tablespoons butter*	⅛ *teaspoon pepper*
4 *tablespoons red wine*	

1. Shred cabbage. Mince onion. Peel and cube apple.

2. Melt butter in a large pan over moderate heat. Lightly brown onion. Add cabbage and toss to combine with onion. Turn for a minute or two. Add apple and all other ingredients. Bring to boil. Reduce heat and simmer 45 minutes or until almost all liquid has cooked out.

This vegetable reheats beautifully. It has an affinity for pork and duck.

⅓ BUTTERED GREEN CABBAGE

SERVES 4 TO 6 · 15 TO 20 MINUTES

1 *small cabbage*	*About ¼ teaspoon lemon*
Boiling water just to cover	*juice*
2 *tablespoons butter*	*Freshly ground black*
Pinch caraway seeds	*pepper*
½ *teaspoon salt*	

1. Shred cabbage finely. Cook uncovered in water over moderate heat 5 to 8 minutes. Cabbage should be tender but crisp. Drain.

2. Melt butter in skillet. Add cabbage, caraway seeds, and salt, stirring until butter is well mixed with cabbage.

3. Remove from heat. Mix in lemon juice to taste. Add extra salt if it is needed. Grind a little pepper over cabbage before serving.

It is better to undercook than overcook the cabbage in this recipe. You may add a bit of sugar, but just a very little, when the cabbage is mixed with the butter. Good with pork, veal, beef, and fish.

⅓ Variation · SAUTÉED GREEN CABBAGE WITH SOUR CREAM

15 TO 20 MINUTES

1. Follow Step 1.

2. In Step 2, after butter is melted, sauté 4 minced scallions with tops for 2 minutes. Proceed with remainder of step, adding ½ teaspoon of prepared mustard.

3. Follow Step 3, but add only a few drops of lemon juice and 2 tablespoons of sour cream.

118

❧ CAULIFLOWER, ITALIAN STYLE

SERVES 6 · 35 MINUTES

1 *medium-sized cauliflower*   2 *tablespoons grated*
½ *teaspoon salt*   *Parmesan cheese*
1 *clove garlic*   1½ *tablespoons olive oil*
1 *tablespoon chopped parsley*

1. Prepare cauliflower for cooking. Divide into flowerlets. Have ready boiling water.
2. Steam vegetable by placing on rack in steamer or pot, above an inch of water. Sprinkle with salt and cover. Or boil by cooking in boiling, salted water barely to cover. Steam or boil 15 to 20 minutes until just tender. Drain.
3. Mince garlic, chop parsley, and grate cheese. Heat oil in frying-pan. Cook garlic and parsley slowly 2 minutes. Add cauliflower and turn in oil 2 minutes. Allow it to colour slightly. Remove from heat. Sprinkle with cheese while vegetable is still hot.

❧ Variation · CAULIFLOWER SALAD

SERVES 6 · 30 MINUTES

1. Follow Steps 1 and 2.
2. Place cauliflower in bowl. While it is still warm, pour over 5 tablespoons of oil. Toss to coat each piece. Sprinkle with 2 tablespoons of wine vinegar, 1 tablespoon of fresh chopped chervil or ½ teaspoon of dried chervil, and ⅛ teaspoon of pepper. Toss once more. Serve warm or chilled.

❧ PURÉED CARROTS

SERVES 4 · 35 MINUTES

Boiling, salted water   1 *tablespoon butter*
½ *pound carrots (about 5 or*   3 *tablespoons raw rice*
   6 *medium-sized ones)*   2 *tablespoons butter*
2 *teaspoons sugar*   *Milk if needed*

1. Have ready boiling, salted water to cover carrots.
2. Slice carrots thinly. Add to water with sugar, butter, and rice. Cover and cook over medium heat until very soft, about 20 minutes. Drain off liquid. Press carrots and rice through a food mill or sieve.
3. Place puréed mixture in a skillet with 2 tablespoons of butter over hot fire and stir to dry purée somewhat. Add a little milk, if it is needed for the consistency you prefer.
4. Serve hot.

Here are carrots with a definite sweet-potato taste. Fine with veal, pork, and poultry.

❧ CARROTS SAUTERNE

SERVES 4 · 25 MINUTES

3 *medium-sized carrots*	1½ *tablespoons butter*
½ *cup water*	1 *tablespoon brown sugar*
¼ *cup Sauterne or any white wine*	¼ *teaspoon salt*

1. Cut carrots julienne style (like matchsticks).
2. Combine water, wine, butter, sugar, and salt and bring to boil.
3. Add carrots, bring to boil, and simmer covered until tender and liquid evaporates. Watch carefully towards end of cooking time and occasionally baste carrots with liquid to glaze them.

❧ VICHY CARROTS

SERVES 3 TO 4 · 30 MINUTES

4 *large carrots*	1 *tablespoon butter*
½ *teaspoon salt*	1 *tablespoon chopped parsley*
2 *teaspoons sugar*	

1. Scrape carrots and slice them. Add to boiling water to barely cover with salt, sugar and butter.

2. Cook over medium heat 20 minutes or until soft and most of liquid has evaporated. Uncover and increase heat to help evaporation. Turn carrots to glaze. Guard against burning. When no liquid is left, carrots are done.

3. Chop parsley. Sprinkle it on carrots and serve.

❧ Variation I · GLAZED CARROT STICKS

SERVES 3 TO 4 · 30 MINUTES

1. Use carrots of same size. Cut off a piece at thin end. Slit carrot lengthwise into 4 pieces.

2. Follow above recipe.

❧ Variation II · GLAZED WHITE ONIONS

SERVES 3 TO 4 · 35 MINUTES

Use 8 to 10 small white onions, whole.
Use chicken broth instead of water, and only 1 teaspoon of sugar. Follow above recipe. Omit parsley.

❧ CUCUMBERS MAÎTRE D'HÔTEL

SERVES 4 · 20 MINUTES

1 *cup boiling water*	3 *large firm cucumbers*
½ *teaspoon salt*	1 *tablespoon butter*
1 *tablespoon chopped parsley*	⅛ *teaspoon freshly ground*
1 *tablespoon chopped chives*	*black pepper*
or dill	

1. Have ready boiling salted water. Chop parsley and chives or dill.

2. Peel cucumbers. Cut into quarters lengthwise. Remove seeds. Slice into 1-inch sections. Boil, covered, over moderate heat until tender, about 10 minutes. Drain. Return to pan.

121

3. Toss cucumbers in pan over low heat to remove moisture. Add butter, herbs, and pepper. Toss again for 1 minute. Correct seasoning if necessary. Serve hot.

Of course, this belongs with fish. It's also good with curries.

⅄ AUBERGINE PANCAKES

SERVES 4 TO 6 · 30 MINUTES

Boiling water to cover	*½ teaspoon salt*
1 small aubergine	*¼ teaspoon dried tarragon*
1 egg yolk	*Pinch pepper*
3 or 4 tablespoons flour	*2 tablespoons oil*
½ teaspoon baking powder	

1. Have boiling water ready, as aubergine discolours if left standing.
2. Pare and cube aubergine. Cook until it is tender enough to mash, about 10 minutes. Drain well and mash. If it seems too watery, pour off some of the liquid.
3. Stir in unbeaten egg yolk until it is well combined with vegetable. Stir in remaining ingredients except oil.
4. Heat oil in a large pan. Drop large spoonfuls of mixture into oil. Flatten out pancakes slightly with back of spoon. Brown them on both sides over medium heat. Drain them on paper towels and serve them hot.

Don't hesitate to serve these pancakes to persons known to be hostile to aubergine; you will make converts to this regal-looking vegetable. Deep-fry the pancakes if you wish. Of course lamb is the perfect meat to offer with aubergine, but I have tried it with everything but pork and found it delicious.

⅄ AUBERGINE, TOMATO, AND ONION SAUTÉ

SERVES 4 TO 6 · 1¾ TO 2¼ HOURS

2 large onions	*3 medium-sized tomatoes*
1 large aubergine	*2 tablespoons chopped parsley*

2 *tablespoons olive oil*   1 *teaspoon brown sugar*
½ *teaspoon dried tarragon*   3 *dashes Tabasco*
1 *teaspoon salt*

1. Dice onions. Peel and cube aubergine. Peel and slice tomatoes, saving juice. Chop parsley.
2. Heat oil in a skillet over moderate heat. Sauté onions until light brown. Add aubergine, tomatoes and their juice, parsley, tarragon, salt, sugar, and Tabasco. Mix. Add no water. Cover and simmer for 1½ to 2 hours. Stir occasionally. Correct seasoning.

Prepare this ahead of time if you wish, and either reheat it before it is to be used, or serve it cold as a salad with a little lemon juice squeezed over it.

⅙ KASHA (BUCKWHEAT GROATS)

SERVES 4 · 20 MINUTES

1 *cup medium buckwheat*   1 *teaspoon salt*
 groats   1 *egg*
2 *cups boiling water or*   1 *tablespoon butter or*
 chicken broth   *chicken fat*

1. Have ready boiling water or chicken broth. Add salt to water. Add no salt if broth is salted.
2. Heat a large skillet over moderate heat. Place buckwheat in pan and add unbeaten egg, stirring constantly and briskly with a fork until each grain is dry and separate.
3. Add liquid slowly. Stir and bring to a boil. Cover and cook slowly until liquid has been absorbed, about 15 minutes.
4. Add butter or fat and mix with two forks to fluff up.

An excellent dish with pot roast and gravy. A fine substitute for potatoes or rice.

⅌ CURRIED LENTILS

SERVES 6 · PREPARATION 1¾ HOURS
SOAKING OVERNIGHT

½ *pound* (1 *cup*) *lentils*	1 *tablespoon curry powder*
3 *medium-sized onions*	½ *teaspoon salt*
4 *to* 5 *tablespoons butter or*	*A little water or stock only if*
dripping	*needed*

1. Wash and soak lentils overnight in cold water.
2. Slice or dice onions. Melt butter in a large skillet. When it is hot, add onions. Sprinkle curry powder and salt over onions, and cook slowly 10 minutes.
3. Drain lentils and mix in. Cover and simmer until they are soft but still keep their shape, about 1½ hours. If they become too dry to cook without burning, add a little water or stock. Stir occasionally.
4. Serve hot.

In this Scotch recipe, lentils and curry have a definite affinity for each other. This dish is excellent with lamb. Try it with smoked tongue too.

⅌ MUSHROOMS AND ONIONS IN WINE SAUCE

SERVES 4 · 25 MINUTES

8 *small white onions*	½ *bay leaf*
½ *pound medium-sized*	½ *teaspoon salt*
mushrooms	*Pinch cayenne*
2 *tablespoons chopped parsley*	¼ *cup chicken stock*
3 *or* 4 *tablespoons butter*	2 *tablespoons dry white wine*
½ *tablespoon flour*	

1. Peel onions. Wipe off mushrooms with damp cloth, cutting off a narrow slice from each stem end. Chop parsley, reserving half of it for garnish.

124

2. Melt butter over low heat in a large skillet. Sauté onions 8 minutes without permitting them to brown.

3. Add whole mushrooms and turn them 1 minute in butter to coat. Sprinkle them with flour, and stir.

4. Add parsley, bay leaf, salt, cayenne, and stock. Stir to blend well; bring to a boil; cover and cook slowly about 10 or 12 minutes until onions are tender. Stir occasionally.

5. Add wine; cover and cook 1 minute. Remove bay leaf.

6. Place vegetables on a hot serving dish and sprinkle them with reserved parsley.

⅍ NOODLE PUDDING KEREKES

SERVES 6 · 1¼ TO 1½ HOURS

2 *quarts boiling water*   3 *eggs*
  containing 2 teaspoons salt   ¾ *teaspoon salt*
5 *ounces egg noodle,* ½ *inch*   ⅛ *teaspoon white pepper*
  wide   *Good pinch nutmeg*
4 *tablespoons butter*

1. Place noodles in boiling salted water. Bring back to a boil and cook noodles 8 minutes. Pour them into a strainer and rinse well with cold water. Drain.

2. Melt butter and stir it into noodles.

3. Add seasonings to eggs, beat eggs, and combine with noodle mixture.

4. Butter heavily the bottom and sides of a 9- or 10-inch skillet. Stir noodles well and place in pan. Cover and let cook over low heat 30 minutes. Slip spatula around sides and bottom to loosen pudding so as to prevent possible sticking. Continue to cook until pudding is brown and crisp on underside. Loosen with spatula and turn over to brown other side. The cooking of the pudding should take about 1 hour to 1 hour and 15

minutes. This is a fine substitute for potatoes or rice when you are serving a pot roast or stew. Spoon some gravy or sauce over each portion, or pass the gravy in a dish.

⅙ BOILED POTATOES

1 POTATO PER SERVING · 25 MINUTES

1 *medium-sized potato per*   1 *small onion*
  serving

1. Have ready boiling, salted water.
2. Leave skins on and scrub potatoes well. Peel onion and place with potatoes in water to cover. The onion will flavour old potatoes and need not be used with new ones. Cook until potatoes are just tender, about 25 minutes.
2. Hold cover over pot slightly pushed back and pour off liquid. Tilt pot away from you to avoid steam. Do not remove cover, or remove potatoes from pot, or heat will be lost. Make sure all water has been drained off; some is sometimes left in the lid and pours back on to potatoes. Discard onion. Shake pan gently. Return it with potatoes to same burner, with heat turned off, and cover partially. Let potatoes steam 2 or 3 minutes. To peel them, remove one at a time, but return them to pot to complete steaming.

Although this is not a basic cookery book, I have included this recipe because potatoes are often spoiled by improper cooking. If you are not pressed for time when making mashed potatoes, cook whole with peel on and then mash.

⅙ Variation I · PARSLEY POTATOES

SERVES 6 · 30 MINUTES

1. Use 12 small potatoes, and hot salted chicken broth in place of water. Follow all steps. Allow 15 to 20 minutes for boiling.

2. Add to peeled steamed potatoes 1 tablespoon of butter in bits, and toss them lightly until they are coated. Sprinkle them with 1 tablespoon of chopped fresh parsley. Serve them at once.

Of course parsley potatoes are the classic partner for fish, but new potatoes prepared in this manner are a delight with any entrée. These may be scraped before cooking.

❧ Variation II · CHIVE POTATOES

SERVES 6 · 30 MINUTES

1. Omit onion and cook like Parsley Potatoes. Instead of parsley, sprinkle with 2 tablespoons of chopped fresh chives.

❧ Variation III · POTATOES MAÎTRE D'HÔTEL

2 POTATOES PER SERVING · 1¼ HOURS

1. Boil medium-sized potatoes and peel them. Slice them while they are still hot into ¼-inch rounds.
2. Cover with boiling milk; season with salt and white pepper to taste. Cook them slowly. Turn them now and then and guard against overboiling milk. When milk has been absorbed, serve potatoes with a liberal sprinkling of chopped parsley.

❧ LYONNAISE POTATOES

SERVES 4 · 25 MINUTES

Boiling salted water to cover	*2 medium-sized onions*
potatoes	*Salt*
4 medium-sized potatoes	*⅛ teaspoon pepper*
2 tablespoons oil	*1 teaspoon chopped parsley*
1 tablespoon butter	

1. Have ready boiling, salted water. Peel potatoes, cut them into large cubes, and cook until almost soft.

2. Pour off liquid. Shake pan quickly. Cover. Return to burner with heat off. Push back cover a bit and let potatoes steam for 2 minutes.

3. Heat oil and butter in a skillet. Add potato cubes and brown them uncovered over medium heat.

4. Cut onions into small dice. Turn potato cubes over. Add diced onion, pushing onion between potatoes. Cook until both are browned. Chop parsley.

5. When potatoes are ready to be served, sprinkle them with pepper and parsley, and salt if necessary.

❧ POTATO PANCAKES ↖

12 MEDIUM-SIZED PANCAKES · 30 TO 35 MINUTES

4 *large potatoes*	$\frac{1}{8}$ *teaspoon white pepper*
1 *small onion*	1 *egg*
2 *to 3 tablespoons flour*	2 *tablespoons or more bland*
$\frac{1}{2}$ *teaspoon salt*	*oil*

1. Grate potatoes on a fine grater or put them through the special potato grater of a food chopper. Pour off liquid that accumulates, pressing it out with the back of a wooden spoon. Grate in onion finely. Add flour, salt, pepper, and unbeaten egg. Mix together well.

2. Heat oil in a large frying-pan over medium heat. When oil is hot, drop in spoonfuls of batter, using wooden spoon, and flatten them out. Pancakes should not touch. Reduce heat a little after 1 or 2 minutes and cook until undersides of pancakes are crisp and medium brown. Flip them over. Turn up heat to medium for a minute or so to develop crispness and then lower heat as before. Finish cooking.

3. Serve pancakes with gravy, sugar, sour cream, or apple sauce.

As oil is used up, add extra oil to pan, heating it before adding another batch of pancakes. If necessary, the potatoes may be grated 30 minutes before the pancakes are to be made, the accumulated liquid poured off, and the juice of 1 lemon mixed in well. Then they should be covered and refrigerated. After they are removed from the refrigerator, any accumulated liquid should be poured off before you proceed to make the pancakes.

⚜ POTATO PUDDING

SERVES 4 · $1\frac{1}{4}$ TO $1\frac{1}{2}$ HOURS

3 *tablespoons butter*	1 *teaspoon salt*
1 *small onion*	$\frac{1}{4}$ *teaspoon white pepper*
4 *large potatoes*	2 *eggs*
4 *tablespoons flour*	

1. Use a heavy 6-inch frying-pan. Grease the bottom and sides with 1 tablespoon of butter.
2. Grate onion coarsely. Peel and grate potatoes with a fine grater as for potato pancakes. Pour off liquid that accumulates.
3. Mix in a bowl onion, potatoes, flour, salt, and pepper. Break eggs at edge of mixture and beat them lightly with a fork. Then mix with potatoes.
4. Pour mixture into prepared pan. Poke 2 tablespoons of butter, in small pieces, into pudding. Cover pan tightly. Place it over moderate heat for 2 minutes. Reduce to very low heat. Use an asbestos pad over the burner if heat is not low enough to prevent scorching. Cook for 30 minutes without peeking. Bottom of pudding should be medium to dark brown. Turn and cook other side for 30 minutes, covered. If it is brown and crusty, it is done. If not, let it cook a while longer.
5. Cut pudding into 4 wedges. Serve it piping hot or with meat gravy.

Also good with sugar over it, or with a spoonful of sour cream or apple sauce. Should the recipe be increased, be sure the pan used is a shallow one.

⅛ SKILLET POTATOES

SERVES 4 · 50 TO 60 MINUTES

2 *large potatoes*	½ *teaspoon salt*
2 *medium-sized onions*	¼ *teaspoon pepper*
2 *tablespoons butter*	Cold water
¼ *teaspoon paprika*	*Paprika for dusting*

1. Slice potatoes and onions very thinly.
2. Melt 1 tablespoon butter in a medium-sized skillet. When it is hot, add a single layer of potatoes. Brown them well over moderate heat.
3. Cover potatoes with a layer of onions. Sprinkle them with a little of the paprika, salt, and pepper. Alternate layers of potatoes and onions until all the slices are used up. Sprinkle seasoning over each pair of layers until all seasoning has been used up.
4. Add water halfway to top. Dot with 1 tablespoon of butter. Dust with additional paprika. Cover potatoes and cook them slowly for about 30 minutes. Uncover to brown them, and cook until all liquid has evaporated, about another 15 minutes.

I serve this often with cubed or minute steaks to teenagers. It's a tasty, hearty dish, and substitutes beautifully for scalloped potatoes.

⅛ BOILED RICE

SERVES 4 TO 6 · 25 MINUTES

4 *cups water*	*Hot water for rinsing rice*
½ *teaspoon salt*	1 *tablespoon butter*
1 *cup long-grain rice*	(*optional*)

1. Add salt to water and bring to a boil. Add rice and cook vigorously 18 minutes from time water starts to boil again.

130

2. Drain rice into a strainer. Rinse rice with hot water, stirring gently with a fork. Let it drain well. Return it to pot, place over burner with heat off, and cover partially to steam a minute or so.

3. Mix in butter if you wish.

This method of cooking rice is most suitable in a dish where cooked rice is combined with other ingredients and additional cooking is called for. Rinsing may be done with cold water in that case.

Variation · SPANISH RICE

SERVES 4 TO 6 · 35 MINUTES

1. Follow Steps 1 and 2. Omit Step 3.
2. While rice cooks, sauté ¼ pound of sliced, fresh mushrooms in 1 tablespoon of hot butter for 5 minutes. Mince 1 small green pepper. Skin 2 medium-sized tomatoes. Quarter them, remove seeds; save juice for other use. Set aside fleshy shells.
3. Melt 2 tablespoons of butter in small pan. Cook pepper over low heat, uncovered, 3 minutes. Add sautéed mushrooms and cook 2 minutes. Add tomato pieces and sauté 3 minutes. Season with ¼ teaspoon of salt and ⅛ teaspoon of pepper.
4. Combine vegetables and rice, tossing with 2 forks.
5. Serve rice hot.

An excellent rice dish for serving with fried fish, or with any meat that is served in its natural, unthickened juices. Leftover rice reheats well in the top of a double boiler. If fresh mushrooms are not handy, use 2 or 3 ounces of tinned mushrooms. In this case, drain them and add after the green pepper.

⅍ RICE MILANESE

SERVES 4 TO 6 · 35 MINUTES

1 *small onion*	⅛ *teaspoon white pepper*
1 *tablespoon oil*	*Pinch powdered saffron*
1 *cup unwashed long-grain*	*diluted in 1 tablespoon*
rice	*water*
2 *cups hot chicken broth*	3 *tablespoons butter*
2 *tablespoons white wine*	4 *tablespoons Parmesan*
Salt	*cheese*

1. Use a heavy frying-pan with a tight cover. Mince onion. Heat oil over low heat. Add onion and rice and cook for 8 minutes until they are slightly coloured. Turn rice several times with spatula to colour it evenly.

2. Slowly add chicken broth, wine, salt if needed, and pepper. Stir. Turn up heat and bring to a vigorous boil for 30 seconds. Reduce heat, cover, and cook without stirring over low heat for 15 minutes. Turn off heat. Let rice steam for about 5 minutes.

3. Dissolve saffron in hot water. Stir it into rice, using 2 forks to mix and lift rice.

4. Just before serving, sprinkle rice with melted butter and grated cheese.

⅍ RICE PIEMONTAISE

SERVES 4 TO 6 · 35 MINUTES

1 *small onion*	2 *to* 2½ *cups hot chicken*
1 *tablespoon oil*	*broth*
1 *cup unwashed long-grain*	1 *tablespoon butter*
rice	4 *tablespoons grated*
¼ *teaspoon powdered saffron*	*Parmesan cheese*
(if available)	

132

1. Dice onion. Heat oil in a large frying-pan over low heat. Sauté onion and rice slowly for 10 minutes, until light brown. Turn 2 or 3 times with spatula.

2. Dissolve saffron in 2 tablespoons of hot broth. Stir this into rice.

3. Add slowly a half cup of hot broth. Stir with a wooden spoon. Cover and cook over low heat until liquid almost evaporates. Add another half cup of broth and repeat process. Continue this until rice is tender and liquid is absorbed—about 18 minutes. The rice will need 2 full cups of broth; don't use any more unless the rice needs more cooking.

4. Fluff up rice with 2 forks. Stir in butter that has been cut into bits. Mix with forks. Stir in grated cheese and mix. Serve rice hot.

A terrific rice dish, well worth the watching it requires.

℣ RICE PILAF

SERVES 4 TO 6 · 25 MINUTES

1 *small onion*	2 *cups hot seasoned chicken*
1 *tablespoon oil*	*broth, fresh, tinned, or*
1 *cup long-grained rice,*	*made with 2 chicken*
unwashed	*bouillon cubes and 2 cups*
	hot water

1. Use a large 9- or 10-inch skillet with a cover.
2. Mince onion. Heat oil over low heat. Sauté onion and rice, without browning onion, about 5 minutes. Turn with a spatula twice for even colouring.
3. Turn off heat. Pour hot broth slowly over rice. Stir to mix. Turn on medium heat and bring to a boil. Cover and cook 15 minutes over very low heat without stirring. The liquid should be almost completely absorbed and each grain whole, not mushy.

4. Turn off heat. Let rice steam, covered, 5 to 8 minutes. Uncover and fluff up rice with two forks. Serve it hot.

If it cannot be served immediately, rice prepared in this fashion will not spoil except to cool off a bit. Leftover rice may be reheated the next day with a bit of butter over hot water or in a pan directly over low heat. I find this the easiest way to prepare rice, as well as the tastiest.

Variations

RICE PILAF WITH GREEN PEAS

Place 1 cup of cooked peas over rice, without stirring, 3 minutes before rice is done. When it is done, add 2 tablespoons of melted butter and fluff up rice with 2 forks. Cover and allow pilaf to steam on burner, with heat off, 5 to 8 minutes.

RICE PILAF WITH GREEN PEAS AND SWEET RED PEPPER

Proceed with green peas as above. When rice is done, add 3 tablespoons of raw minced sweet red pepper along with the melted butter, and fluff up with forks. Cover and let pilaf steam.

RICE PILAF WITH GREEN PEPPER

Sauté 1 minced small green pepper lightly without browning in 1 tablespoon of butter. Add with 2 tablespoons of melted butter to cooked rice. Fluff up rice and let it steam.

RICE PILAF WITH MUSHROOMS

Sauté $\frac{1}{4}$ pound of sliced mushrooms in 1 tablespoon of butter. Add this to cooked rice with another tablespoon of melted butter. Fluff up rice and let it steam.

RICE PILAF WITH RAISINS

Add $\frac{1}{2}$ cup of raisins to rice with stock before cooking. (If raisins are hard, soften them in hot water, drain, and dry.) When rice is done, add 1 or 2 tablespoons melted butter. Fluff up rice and let it steam.

134

RICE PILAF WITH RAISINS AND ALMONDS

Add ¼ cup of softened raisins with stock before cooking. When rice is done, stir in ¼ cup of blanched, slivered, and toasted almonds with 2 tablespoons of melted butter; fluff up rice and let it steam.

RICE PILAF WITH RAISINS AND PINE NUTS

Follow directions in recipe above.

RICE PILAF WITH SAFFRON

Add ½ teaspoon of powdered saffron and 1 small bay leaf at same time as stock. Stir well and cook. Remove bay leaf. When rice is done, add 2 tablespoons of melted butter. Fluff up rice and let it steam.

RICE PILAF WITH TOMATOES

Skin, seed, and mince 2 small tomatoes. Add these to cooked rice with 2 tablespoons of melted butter. Fluff up rice and let it steam.

In all these recipes for Rice Pilaf, I have given the minimum amount of melted butter for final mixing. You may add more butter if you prefer.

⟍⟋ SPAGHETTI MILANESE

SERVES 8 · 30 MINUTES

1 *pound spaghetti*	2 *tablespoons cooked tongue*
4 *to 5 quarts boiling water*	2 *tablespoons cooked*
1½ *tablespoons salt*	*mushrooms*
4 *tablespoons butter*	1 *tablespoon oil*
4 *tablespoons grated Gruyère*	¼ *teaspoon white pepper*
cheese	*Pinch nutmeg*
4 *tablespoons grated*	*Salt to taste*
Parmesan cheese	2 *cups* TOMATO SAUCE
2 *tablespoons lean cooked*	
ham	

1. Add salt to water in a pan. Have it boiling rapidly. Set out a large strainer. Melt butter. Grate cheeses. Cut meats and mushrooms into short, thin strips; warm them up in a few tablespoons of tomato sauce.

2. Add oil to boiling water. Drop spaghetti in without breaking it. From the time water returns to a boil, cook spaghetti vigorously, uncovered, 10 minutes. Test it by tasting a strand. It should have lost its starchy look, and be firm and edible. If it is not done, cook it another minute and test again. Boiling more than 12 to 13 minutes usually makes spaghetti too soft.

3. Pour spaghetti immediately into strainer, and rinse quickly with cold water. Let it drain; shake strainer to make sure no water remains. Return spaghetti to pot over same burner, with heat off. Add butter and toss with 2 forks to mix. Add cheese a little at a time; toss to blend. Mix in meats and mushrooms. Season with pepper and nutmeg, and salt if any is needed.

4. Serve spaghetti on a hot platter. Top with some of the sauce. Pass remaining sauce and grated cheese.

✑ CHOPPED SPINACH

SERVES 4 TO 6 · 20 MINUTES

2 *pounds fresh spinach, well* *washed*	4 *tablespoons light cream*
1 *tablespoon butter*	½ *teaspoon sugar or more to*
Salt to taste	*taste*
	Pinch nutmeg

1. Cook washed spinach without water in a covered pan over medium-low heat 5 or 6 minutes or until spinach is wilted. Drain it well. Chop it fine.

2. Melt butter in a skillet. When it is hot, add spinach. Add salt. Sauté, stirring until most of moisture leaves spinach. Add cream, sugar, and nutmeg. Mix. Warm up without boiling.

3. Serve spinach hot.

136

CREAMED SPINACH

SERVES 4 TO 6 · 25 MINUTES

2 *packets frozen chopped*　　½ *cup sour cream*
　spinach　　　　　　　　　¼ *teaspoon salt*
1 *cup water*　　　　　　　　⅛ *teaspoon freshly ground*
1 *teaspoon salt*　　　　　　　*black pepper*
1 *tablespoon butter*　　　　　*Pinch nutmeg (optional)*
1 *tablespoon flour*

1. In a saucepan, cook frozen spinach in boiling salted water according to directions on packet. When it is tender, drain it, pressing out liquid. (Save liquid for other cooking use.)

2. Return spinach to saucepan; keep it warm.

3. In a small skillet, melt butter. Blend in flour with a wire whisk over low heat. Away from fire, add sour cream a little at a time, and salt; whisk sauce until it comes to a boil.

4. Mix sauce into spinach over low heat. Add pepper, nutmeg, and additional salt if it is needed. Serve spinach immediately. Keep it warm if necessary by setting saucepan in hot water.

SQUASH CREOLE

SERVES 6 · 50 MINUTES

3 *large tomatoes*　　　　　　3 *tablespoons oil*
1 *large onion*　　　　　　　1 *tablespoon butter*
1 *garlic clove (optional)*　　 1½ *teaspoons brown sugar*
2 *green peppers*　　　　　　¾ *teaspoon salt*
3 *medium-sized yellow*　　　⅛ *to* ¼ *teaspoon pepper*
　summer squash　　　　　　¼ *to* ½ *teaspoon dried*
　　　　　　　　　　　　　　tarragon

1. Peel tomatoes and mince them, saving juice. Mince onion and garlic. Seed peppers; cut them julienne (into matchlike strips). Cut unpeeled squash into slices ¼ inch to ⅜ inch thick.

2. Heat oil and butter in a large skillet. Add onion, garlic, and green peppers. Cook over medium-low heat 5 or 6 minutes.

3. Add squash slices. Sprinkle them with sugar and brown them lightly on both sides.

4. Mix in tomatoes with their juice, and seasoning. Cook slowly, covered, 30 minutes. Stir several times. Add no water unless tomatoes are very dry. Taste to adjust seasoning.

This is a fine vegetable stew to accompany meat and fish dishes that are prepared with no sauces of their own. It goes with rice as Jack with Jill.

ϗ Variation I

For BABY MARROW CREOLE, replace squash with the same quantity of baby marrow, and cook it unpeeled. Proceed with recipe.

ϗ Variation II

For AUBERGINE CREOLE, replace squash with a 'large aubergine, peeled and cubed. Proceed with recipe.

ϗ MASHED SWEET POTATOES WITH SHERRY

SERVES 4 TO 6 · 30 MINUTES

6 *medium-sized sweet potatoes*	2 *tablespoons butter*
Boiling, unsalted water to cover	2 *or more tablespoons sherry*
	Milk
½ *teaspoon salt*	2 *tablespoons brown sugar*
	Grated rind of 1 *orange*

1. Have boiling water ready. Scrub potatoes well. Cook them in water until they are tender. Drain off liquid. Steam them for 2 minutes. Peel and rice or mash them. Sprinkle them with salt. Return potatoes to burner.

2. Make a well in potatoes. Drop in butter and let it melt over low heat. Turn off heat. Mix butter with potatoes. Make another well. Pour in 2 tablespoons of sherry. Let this heat for a few seconds. Mix it with potatoes. More liquid will be needed, so taste potatoes to determine whether to add milk or more sherry; too much sherry can be overwhelming. Add sugar.

3. Beat potatoes with a rotary beater or fork until they are light. Sprinkle them with grated orange rind.

Delicious with ham, of course, and with turkey, chicken, or duck prepared without wine sauces. If you have a large enough double boiler, cook the sweet potatoes in the top, and keep them warm by placing the top over hot water.

ɣⱻ MARROW PATTIES

SERVES 4 TO 6 · 25 MINUTES

2 *medium-sized marrows*	¼ *teaspoon powdered*
1 *small onion*	*tarragon*
1 *egg, slightly beaten*	*Salt and pepper to taste*
2 *or 3 tablespoons flour*	1 *tablespoon oil*
	2 *tablespoons butter*

1. Shred unpeeled marrows, using a coarse grater. Grate onion coarsely. ·

2. Combine all ingredients except oil and butter. Add only enough flour to make a mixture that holds together.

3. Heat oil and butter in a skillet. Drop the mixture, a tablespoon at a time, into the hot fat. Flatten down with the back of a spoon. Cook patties uncovered over medium heat until they are a crisp brown. Turn and brown the other side. Drain them on paper towels. Serve them hot.

If you usually find this vegetable too dull for your taste, try it this unusual way. It's simple to prepare; the grating goes very

139

fast. Don't be alarmed by the unappetizing look of the grated product. It cooks through nicely, retaining a pleasing crispness. Prepare the mixture a little ahead of time if you wish, but refrigerate it until you are ready to cook it. Fine with meat, fish, or poultry.

⅓ SHREDDED MARROW WITH SOUR CREAM

SERVES 6 · 20 MINUTES

2 *pounds marrow*	*Salt and pepper*
Boiling water barely	*Few drops lime or lemon*
to cover	*juice*
1 *tablespoon butter*	1 *cup sour cream*
¼ *teaspoon powdered*	*Paprika*
tarragon	

1. Have ready boiling water. Coarsely grate unpeeled marrows. Boil rapidly for 5 minutes. Drain thoroughly.
2. Add butter in bits and stir to melt it.
3. Sprinkle over tarragon, a cautious amount of salt and pepper, and the lime or lemon juice.
4. Add gradually enough sour cream to moisten the marrow well. Stir to blend with seasonings. Heat gently so as not to curdle the cream.
5. Serve hot with a dusting of paprika.

Marrow prepared this way makes a fine accompaniment to grilled lamb chops, chicken, and steak, and sautéed pork chops and hamburgers. It's fine with meats or fish that have no sauces or gravies of their own.

SALADS WITH ZEST

I F you start with crisp dry greens and/or other salad materials, and add just enough good dressing, you are almost assured of a fine salad. An extra touch—snips of a fresh herb, a pinch of special seasoning, perhaps a dash of flavouring, or a pretty garnish that contributes to the taste—can make it a masterpiece. Try some chopped fresh tarragon, or a bit of dried tarragon with green, fish, or chicken salads; basil or oregano with tomato or beans; chopped chives with potato or egg salads. Garnish a plain green salad with a few chopped pistachios and serve with pork.

Rinse lettuce (other large-leaved greens too) under cold running water. Set it core end down in a colander or drainer for several hours to drip and dry. The dish drainer is perfect for this. If you are pressed for time, place the lettuce in a wire lettuce basket and swing and whirl it to throw off the moisture. This takes energy and never completely dries the greens, so gently finish drying them with a dish towel or paper towel. Don't remove the core or separate the leaves if you'd like to reduce that familiar brown rot. Store it in a covered refrigerator pan. It will crisp beautifully if you don't crowd it.

141

✄ THE TOSSED SALAD

GREENS FOR TOSSED SALAD: lettuce—Boston, iceberg, romaine (Cos), field, Bibb (or any other varieties that may be available); endive, chicory, escarole, watercress, spinach (young leaves).

Choose at least two of these. Use tender chicory, escarole, or endive as they may be too bitter otherwise. Tear or cut it into bite-sized pieces. My family finds 2 large lettuce leaves or the equivalent ample per serving.

HOW TO DRESS THE TOSSED SALAD: Use a FRENCH SALAD DRESSING. (See SAUCES AND SALAD DRESSINGS.)

1. Rub the salad bowl, preferably a wooden one, with garlic, or mash it with salt in the bowl, or use a *chapon* (see SALAD DRESSINGS).

2. Place greens in bowl. Pour oil over them and toss them lightly with a salad fork and spoon until each leaf is lightly coated. Too much oil will wilt the greens. If more than a few drops remain in the bottom of bowl, you've overdone it. If you are not sure how much to use, dress salad with only a little oil at a time, toss the greens, and check to see if they are coated. Keep count of the number of spoonfuls used; you'll need about a third as much vinegar.

3. Add salt, unless it went into the bowl with the garlic, pepper, and vinegar. Toss lightly but thoroughly. Remove *chapon* if salad has one. Serve immediately. If serving must be delayed a few minutes, toss again before serving.

WHEN TO DRESS THE TOSSED SALAD: Dress it immediately before serving to avoid a droopy salad. Leftover salad is unattractive, so make only enough for a meal.

142

⚘ APPLE AND ALMOND SALAD

SERVES 4 TO 6 · 10 MINUTES
3 *large well-flavoured apples*

SHERRY-LEMON DRESSING
3 *tablespoons lemon juice*   3 *tablespoons sugar*
1½ *tablespoons sherry*

¼ *cup almonds, blanched or*   *Romaine or lettuce*
    unblanched   *Paprika*

1. To make SHERRY-LEMON DRESSING, combine lemon juice and sherry. Dissolve sugar in it.
2. Pare, core, and dice apples. Pour dressing over them, and mix.
3. Sliver almonds and add them to apples.
4. Shred romaine finely or select lettuce leaves to serve as cups. Place apples on romaine or in lettuce cups. Dust very lightly with paprika.

⚘ ASPARAGUS VINAIGRETTE

SERVES 6 · PREPARATION 45 MINUTES
CHILLING 1 TO 3 HOURS

3 *pounds asparagus stalks*   *Boiling salted water*

VINAIGRETTE SAUCE
1 *tablespoon chopped scallion*   ½ *cup* FRENCH DRESSING
    (*white part*)   ½ *tablespoon prepared*
1 *tablespoon chopped parsley*   *mustard*
½ *tablespoon chives*

1 *tinned pimento*

143

1. Snap off tough ends of asparagus stalks and discard. Scrape off scales. Wash stalks to remove sand and dirt. Soak them 10 minutes in cold salted water to draw out every particle of sand. Rinse well.

2. Have ready boiling salted water. Lay stalks flat in a large skillet. Barely cover them with water. Cook them covered for 5 minutes over medium heat. Uncover to preserve green colour and cook 10 to 15 minutes or until stalks are tender but firm when stem end is pierced with a fork. Watch towards last few minutes of cooking so they do not become too soft. Drain. When they are cool, chill them in refrigerator.

3. To make vinaigrette sauce, chop scallion, parsley, and chives finely. Combine them in a jar with FRENCH DRESSING and mustard. Shake vigorously. Chill.

4. Slice pimento into 6 strips. Arrange each serving of asparagus on a lettuce leaf. Use chilled salad plates. Garnish with pimento strip. Shake vinaigrette sauce. Pour 1 tablespoonful on each serving.

This dish is often served hot, too. Pass chilled dressing with it.

⅍ GREEN BEANS OREGANO

SERVES 6 · PREPARATION 30 MINUTES
CHILLING 3 HOURS

1 *pound green beans*	½ *clove garlic, crushed*
Boiling water barely to cover	1 *teaspoon oregano powdered*
2 *tablespoons chopped*	*with fingers*
Bermuda or red onion	¼ *teaspoon freshly ground*
6 *tablespoons oil*	*black pepper*
2½ *tablespoons wine vinegar*	*Lettuce leaves*
½ *teaspoon salt*	*Cucumber slices*

1. Have ready boiling water. Cut beans lengthwise in slivers. Cook uncovered 15 to 20 minutes. While beans cook, chop onion. Stir beans once to cook evenly. Drain them thoroughly.

2. Combine oil, vinegar, salt, and crushed garlic in a small jar. Shake vigorously.

3. Pour dressing over beans. Toss them with 2 forks. Add onion with oregano and pepper to beans. Toss salad again. Chill.

4. Serve salad on crisp lettuce leaves. Garnish with chilled cucumber slices if you desire.

A salad to go with fish, lamb, veal, and beef dishes that are not highly seasoned or spiced.

KIDNEY BEAN SALAD

SERVES 4 · PREPARATION 5 MINUTES
CHILLING 2 OR 3 HOURS

1 *tin kidney beans or 2 cups*	*Salt to taste*
cooked kidney beans	*Good dash Tabasco*
1 *small red onion*	$\frac{1}{4}$ *teaspoon oregano*
3 *tablespoons oil*	$\frac{1}{4}$ *teaspoon thyme*
2 *tablespoons wine vinegar*	1 *tablespoon chopped parsley*
1 *small clove garlic, crushed*	

1. Drain beans well. Save liquid for some other use. Mince onion and add it to beans.

2. Combine oil, vinegar, crushed garlic, salt, Tabasco, oregano, and thyme in a jar and shake well. Pour this over beans and turn them to mix in dressing. Taste. They should be rather highly seasoned. Chill salad 2 or 3 hours.

3. Chop parsley and sprinkle it over salad before serving.

⊁ CELERY SALAD

SERVES 8 · PREPARATION 20 MINUTES
CHILLING 4 HOURS

1 *bunch Pascal celery*

MUSTARD CREAM DRESSING

½ *cup medium cream*   *Salt to taste*
1 *tablespoon lemon juice*   *Pinch pepper*
1 *tablespoon prepared*
   mustard

4 *large tomatoes, chilled*

1. Remove leafy part of celery. Cut off bit of root end. Cut ribs into 1-inch-long matchlike strips.
2. To make dressing, combine and stir until well blended the 5 ingredients listed in the recipe. It may need a little more lemon juice.
3. Mix celery sticks and dressing. Chill several hours.
4. Cut tomatoes into thick slices. Heap celery on them and serve.

Mayonnaise may be substituted for the cream, or part mayonnaise and part cream may be used. This is a fine salad to serve with chicken, turkey, duck, veal, beef, and almost everything. Omit tomatoes if accompanying dish has tomato sauce or tomatoes in it.

⊁ COLE SLAW, FRENCH DRESSING

SERVES 6 · PREPARATION 25 MINUTES
CHILLING 2 TO 3 HOURS

1 *small green cabbage*   2 *tablespoons wine vinegar*
1 *small carrot*   1 *tablespoon lemon juice*
½ *green pepper*   1 *teaspoon salt*
3 *tablespoons salad or olive oil*   ¼ *teaspoon sugar*

146

$\frac{1}{8}$ *teaspoon powdered*	$\frac{1}{8}$ *to* $\frac{1}{4}$ *teaspoon freshly*
mustard	*ground black pepper*
	Tomato slices (optional)

1. Prepare 3 cups of cabbage. Quarter, core, and shred it finely. Be sure it is quite dry.
2. Grate carrot coarsely. Shred pepper finely.
3. Combine next 6 ingredients in a small jar and shake well.
4. In a large bowl, mix vegetables and dressing. Toss with 2 forks until well moistened. Chill.
5. Just before serving, toss salad to distribute dressing. Sprinkle with pepper to taste. Serve with border of tomato slices if you wish.

Wet cabbage will dilute dressing, thus spoiling it. After rinsing and quartering, let cabbage drain on rack (I use dish rack) several hours. This may be done a day ahead, in which case the cabbage should be stored when dry in covered refrigerator dish. Three tablespoons of lemon juice may replace the vinegar-juice combination. Don't omit the black pepper, freshly ground. This, like the tossed greens salad, seems to be good with almost everything. Good next day too.

Variation · COLE SLAW SOUR CREAM DRESSING
SERVES 6 · 25 MINUTES

1. Follow Steps 1 and 2.
2. Combine in a small bowl equal quantities of mayonnaise and sour cream about $\frac{1}{3}$ cup each, $\frac{1}{4}$ teaspoon of salt, and 1 tablespoon or more of lemon juice.
3. Omit Step 3. Follow Step 4.
4. Follow Step 5, omitting pepper and tomatoes. Dust lightly with paprika just before serving.

Best when freshly made.

147

✂ CUCUMBER SALAD

SERVES 6 TO 8 · PREPARATION 40 MINUTES
CHILLING 4 HOURS

2 *large, firm cucumbers*
1½ *teaspoons salt*
¼ *cup oil*
1 *tablespoon and 1 teaspoon*
  wine vinegar

2 *teaspoons chopped fresh*
  herb: dill, chervil, or parsley
Freshly ground black
  pepper to taste
Watercress or lettuce leaves

1. Peel cucumbers. Cut them in quarters lengthwise. Remove seeds, and dice them.

2. Place dice in a large, shallow plate. Sprinkle them evenly with salt. Let them stand 30 minutes.

3. Drain off liquid; press out remaining liquid between paper towels. Place cucumbers in a jar. Chop whichever herb you are using.

4. Add oil, vinegar, chopped herb, and pepper. There should be enough dressing for cucumbers to be well moistened by it but not swimming in it. Shake jar very well to distribute dressing. Chill. Shake once or twice before serving.

5. Serve on watercress or lettuce leaf.

   If more dressing is needed, keep same proportion of oil and vinegar. This is equally good as hors d'oeuvre, salad course, or garnish for cold fish.

✂ GUACAMOLE

MAKES 1 CUP · 10 MINUTES

1 *tomato*
1 *ripe avocado pear*
Lime or lemon juice
1 *small onion*

¼ *teaspoon salt*
Small pinch cayenne
½ *teaspoon Worcester Sauce*

148

1. Peel, slice, and seed tomato. Cube it into a chopping bowl.
2. Cut avocado pear in half and remove stone. Brush it immediately with lime or lemon juice. Remove pulp and add it to tomato. Mince onion and add. Chop these together.
3. Season with salt, cayenne. Worcester Sauce, and $\frac{1}{2}$ teaspoon of lime or lemon juice. Mix and taste. It may need more salt and juice.

Use as a dip with corn chips or serve on buttered Melba toast. Use also as a side dish for CHICKEN ENCHILADAS. Stuff celery with this too, or serve it with shredded lettuce, or heap it on tomato slices and garnish with olives.

NIÇOISE SALAD

SERVES 4 · 15 MINUTES

4 tablespoons oil	1½ cups cooked green beans
2 tablespoons vinegar	¼ cup small stoned black
1 tablespoon capers, drained	olives or large ones sliced
¼ teaspoon salt	Romaine or lettuce
Dash Tabasco	2 small tomatoes, chilled
1½ cups cooked potatoes	8 anchovy fillets

1. Place oil, vinegar, capers, salt, and Tabasco in a small jar; shake.
2. Dice potatoes and green beans. Combine with olives. Add dressing and turn gently to mix.
3. Serve at room temperature, or chilled if you prefer.
4. Shred greens and mound salad upon them. Quarter tomatoes. Use tomatoes and anchovies as garnish.

Although this salad offers an excellent opportunity to utilize leftover vegetables, it is fine enough to justify your cooking the vegetables for its own sake. Try it with plain veal or fish dishes.

❦ MARINATED RED ONIONS AND TOMATOES

SERVES 6 · PREPARATION 10 MINUTES
MARINATING 3 HOURS

2 *medium-sized red onions*	½ *teaspoon sugar*
6 *tablespoons oil*	½ *teaspoon salt*
2 *tablespoons wine vinegar*	*Pinch pepper*
3 *tablespoons dry red wine*	3 *tomatoes, well chilled*
¼ *teaspoon dry mustard*	4 *lettuce leaves, shredded*

1. Slice onions and separate slices into rings.
2. Combine in a small jar the next 7 ingredients and shake well.
3. Pour marinade over onions in a bowl and let them stand 3 or more hours. Spoon dressing over onions once or twice. Refrigerate.
4. Fifteen minutes before serving, slice chilled tomatoes into the bowl. Moisten them with the dressing.
5. Arrange onions and tomatoes on a salad platter. Edge with shredded lettuce.

❦ GREEN AND RED PEPPER SALAD

SERVES 4 TO 6 · PREPARATION 25 MINUTES
CHILLING 4 HOURS OR OVERNIGHT

3 *large fleshy green and/or red peppers*	½ *teaspoon salt*
4 *tablespoons olive oil*	⅛ *teaspoon freshly ground black pepper*
4 *teaspoons wine vinegar*	4 *to 6 crisp lettuce leaves*

1. Impale pepper on fork through stem end and turn slowly over medium heat on range until skin blisters and blackens. Peel off with knife.
2. Halve peppers; remove seeds and membranes. Cut into narrow, short strips.
3. Combine oil, vinegar, salt, and pepper. Pour over pepper strips and refrigerate until well chilled.

4. For hors d'oeuvre use, serve as is; for salad, place pepper strips on crisp lettuce leaves.

Prepare this a day ahead if you wish; it seems to be better the next day.

⚥ SPINACH SALAD, SPICY DRESSING

SERVES 4 TO 6 · PREPARATION 20 MINUTES
CHILLING 1 HOUR

1 pound young spinach

SPICY SALAD DRESSING

1 *small egg or* ½ *large one*	2 *tablespoons ketchup*
¼ *teaspoon salt*	½ *cup bland oil*
⅛ *teaspoon dry mustard*	2 *tablespoons wine vinegar*
⅛ *teaspoon paprika*	3 *tablespoons warm water*
½ *teaspoon sugar*	*Garlic*
¼ *teaspoon Worcester Sauce*	

1. Stem, wash, drain, and dry spinach. Let it crisp in refrigerator.

2. To make SPICY SALAD DRESSING, place first 7 ingredients in a bowl. Mix until smooth. Beat in oil and vinegar, alternately and slowly, with a hand or electric beater. Beat in water gradually. For immediate use, add ½ clove of crushed garlic. Otherwise, drop 2 or 3 cloves of garlic into dressing and let them remain overnight or up to 2 days. Then remove garlic. Keep dressing refrigerated.

3. Shred spinach coarsely and place in a salad bowl. Start with ¼ cup dressing and pour in as much dressing as is needed to moisten spinach. Don't saturate salad with dressing. Serve immediately.

An excellent dressing for escarole, chicory, and watercress too. It keeps well for at least 2 weeks under refrigeration.

✄ TOMATO SALAD

SERVES 8 · PREPARATION 25 MINUTES
CHILLING 1 HOUR

1 *egg*	1 *teaspoon salt*
1 *teaspoon chopped fresh chives or dill*	$\frac{1}{8}$ *teaspoon freshly ground black pepper*
1 *teaspoon chopped fresh tarragon or pinch powdered tarragon*	$\frac{1}{4}$ *teaspoon prepared mustard*
1 *teaspoon chopped parsley*	2 *tablespoons wine vinegar*
3 *tablespoons oil*	4 *tomatoes*
	Mixed greens

1. Hard-boil egg. Chop herbs. Pound yolk in a mortar to a smooth paste. Add all other seasonings, except vinegar, and mix thoroughly.
2. Stir in vinegar a little at a time.
3. Cut tomatoes into thick slices and pour dressing over them. Chill 1 hour.
4. Serve tomatoes on mixed greens.

The egg whites may be chopped and sprinkled over the salad if desired.

✄ ITALIAN TOMATO SALAD

SERVES 6 · 10 MINUTES

1 *clove garlic*	3 *romaine leaves*
$\frac{1}{2}$ *teaspoon salt*	3 *lettuce leaves*
3 *tablespoons olive oil*	3 *large firm tomatoes*
1 *tablespoon wine vinegar*	$\frac{1}{4}$ *teaspoon oregano*
$\frac{1}{8}$ *teaspoon freshly ground black pepper*	

152

1. Cut tip off garlic clove; rub the clove in salt until it is mashed and blended with it. Add oil, vinegar, and pepper; blend together.
2. Cut romaine and lettuce into bowl in shreds. Add half the dressing. Toss and arrange as bed for tomatoes.
3. Slice tomatoes and place over greens. Pour remaining dressing over them. Powder oregano with fingers and dust over tomatoes.

Use on an hors d'oeuvre dish with or without greens, or serve with greens as a salad course.

CHOPPED VEGETABLE SALAD, WITHOUT DRESSING

SERVES 4 · 15 MINUTES

3 *tablespoons minced red or Bermuda onion*	2 *tomatoes*
	Salt to taste
1 *tablespoon minced parsley*	*Freshly ground black*
½ *large cucumber*	*pepper to taste*
½ *large green pepper*	*Lemon juice*
2 *ribs celery*	4 *large lettuce leaves*

1. Mince onion and parsley. Peel cucumber. Remove seeds from cucumber and green pepper; cube them. Slice celery thinly.
2. In a chopping bowl, start with onion and parsley and chop them finely. Add cucumber and green pepper and chop them coarsely.
3. Cut tomatoes into the bowl and coarsely chop them. Add sliced celery and seasoning. Add 1 teaspoon of lemon juice, mix, toss and taste. Add more lemon juice if it is needed.
4. Shred lettuce leaves, and arrange chopped vegetables upon them on individual plates.

Our favourite salad when we are dieting.

153

⚜ WATERCRESS-POTATO SALAD

SERVES 6 TO 8 · PREPARATION 40 MINUTES
CHILLING 1 HOUR

5 *medium-sized new potatoes*	¼ *teaspoon salt*
1 *egg*	*Dash Tabasco*
1 *bunch watercress*	2 *teaspoons chopped parsley*
4 *tablespoons dry white wine*	2 *teaspoons chopped chervil,*
6 *tablespoons oil*	*if available*
2 *tablespoons vinegar*	

1. Cook potatoes in boiling, salted water until just tender, about 25 minutes. While potatoes cook, hard-boil egg and shell it. Wash watercress, drain, and dry. When potatoes are done, cool them slightly, then peel and slice them thinly. While they are still warm, sprinkle them with wine.

2. Combine oil, vinegar, salt, and Tabasco in a small jar. Shake well. Pour half the dressing over the potatoes. Turn them gently to mix. Chill them 1 hour.

3. Chop egg. Just before serving, chop parsley and chervil and mix with egg. Pour other half of dressing over watercress. Combine with potatoes.

4. Mound salad in a serving bowl. Sprinkle it with herb-egg mixture.

⚜ PINEAPPLE-COTTAGE CHEESE SALAD

SERVES 4 · 10 MINUTES

FRUIT SALAD DRESSING

3 *tablespoons salad oil*	¼ *teaspoon salt*
1 *tablespoon lemon juice*	*Pinch dry mustard*
1 *tablespoon pineapple juice*	*Pinch white pepper*

4 *tablespoons cottage cheese*	4 *large lettuce leaves*
1 *tablespoon minced scallion,*	4 *tinned pineapple slices*
green and white parts, or	*Paprika*
fresh chives	

1. To make FRUIT SALAD DRESSING, place ingredients in a jar. Shake until dressing is creamy.

2. Blend cheese and minced scallion. Shred lettuce finely and distribute on to 4 salad plates.

3. Place pineapple slices in centre. Top with 1 tablespoon of cheese. Pour 1 tablespoon of dressing over salad. Dust cheese lightly with paprika.

COTTAGE CHEESE FRUIT SALAD

SERVES 6 · PREPARATION 35 MINUTES
CHILLING 4 HOURS

SOUR CREAM FRUIT SALAD DRESSING

½ *pint (1 cup) sour cream*	⅛ *teaspoon sugar*
¼ *cup mayonnaise*	⅛ *teaspoon paprika*
Lime juice to taste	*Pinch salt*

¼ *cup blanched almonds*	6 *fresh pineapple slices (or 6*
1 *pound seedless grapes*	*tinned pineapple slices)*
3 *ripe peaches*	1 *pound cottage cheese*
3 *navel oranges*	*Lettuce*
3 *fresh pears*	*Watercress*
	Paprika

1. Have fruit and plates well chilled before making salad.

2. To make SOUR CREAM FRUIT SALAD DRESSING, combine and blend well all ingredients. Chill dressing in sauceboat.

155

3. Sliver and toast almonds. Wash, drain, and dry the bunch of grapes. Remove the stem from each grape. Peel and slice peaches and oranges. Wash, dry, quarter, and core pears. Core fresh pineapple slices. (Or drain tinned ones.)

4. Use a large, many-sectioned platter if you have one. Place cheese in centre. Keep fruit of same variety together and place in sections. (Or use a large, plain platter. Place cheese in a small bowl in centre. Arrange grapes around bowl and rows of fruit on either side of bowl.) Tuck in lettuce and watercress around edges. Sprinkle paprika and almond slivers over cheese. Pass the dressing.

Thinly-sliced pumpernickel, buttered, goes well with the salad.

❧ SUMMER MEAT SALAD

SERVES 4 · PREPARATION 15 MINUTES
CHILLING 1 HOUR

2 *cups minced boiled beef*
¼ *cup minced red or*
  Bermuda onion
1 *cup diced, tart, unpeeled*
  apple
1 *tablespoon capers*
3 *tablespoons olive oil*

1 *tablespoon vinegar*
¼ *teaspoon salt*
⅛ *teaspoon freshly ground black*
  pepper
2 *cups lettuce, shredded*
2 *chilled ripe tomatoes*
8 *large black olives, chilled*

1. Mince beef and onion. Dice apple.

2. Combine these with capers. Mix in oil and toss. Add vinegar, salt, and pepper. Toss. Chill 1 hour at least.

3. Before serving, taste salad and add salt if it is needed. Shred lettuce, add, and toss. Slice tomatoes. Place salad in a bowl with sliced tomatoes and olives as garnish.

This salad needs a crusty bread like French or Italian.

⚜ CHICKEN SALAD

SERVES 6 · PREPARATION 2½ TO 3 HOURS FOR CHICKEN
(AND CHILLED OVERNIGHT)
SALAD, 40 MINUTES

A 5-pound hen, cut up	*1 cup celery, diced*
2½ to 3 quarts water	*1 tablespoon lemon juice*
1 clove garlic	*½ cup mayonnaise,*
1 carrot	*preferably home-made*
1 rib celery	*1 cup aspic*
1 small onion	*Salt and pepper*
⅓ cup vinegar	*Lettuce leaves*
Pinch thyme	*Black and green olives*

1. Cook hen a day ahead. Simmer it with next seven ingredients until tender. Remove it from broth. Remove skin and bones. Refrigerate meat when it is cool. Return skin and bones to broth. Continue to cook broth until it is reduced by half. Strain it. Cool and refrigerate it for use as aspic next day.

2. Dice chicken and celery.

3. Add lemon juice to mayonnaise, stirring well. Remove fat from aspic. Beat aspic into mayonnaise. When it is smooth, add salt and pepper to taste. Mix with chicken and celery.

4. Arrange salad on lettuce leaves with a garnish of olives.

A supreme chicken salad. Chilled cranberry sauce and hot corn muffins are perfect with the salad.

SAUCES AND SALAD DRESSINGS FOR
MEAT, FISH, EGGS, AND VEGETABLES

⋇ ⋇ ⋇ ⋇ ⋇ ⋇ ⋇ ⋇

⋇ ABOUT SAUCES

WHEN well-prepared and well-matched to the foods they accompany, sauces are a delectable part of many dishes. But with today's emphasis on the slim figure, sauces often have to play a minor rôle. My own feeling about them is twofold. Serve a sauce if the dish can't be enjoyed without it. What is a slice of pot roast without its sauce? Or a steamed pudding? Serve one sauce at a time: the main dish with a sauce, the vegetables without; or the vegetables with a sauce, the main dish without.

Most of the sauces in this book are found elsewhere than in this chapter. Many dishes make their own sauces. In some cases, the sauce appears in the heart of the recipe; in others, it follows it. All are simple and fine. Innumerable variations can be produced by the addition of appropriate herbs, spices, wine, seasoning and flavouring, stock and other liquids, cheese and other ingredients.

In sauce-making, balanced seasoning and smooth texture are most important. No one seasoning should dominate the taste of

158

the sauce, but the flavours of all ingredients should merge in a subtle blend. For a smooth sauce, use a heavy saucepan and a wire whisk. Use the whisk to blend the main ingredients of fat, flour, and liquid. Use it when you add the flour to the melted fat. Use it when you add the liquid. Stir with it until the sauce comes to a boil. Important, too, is the cooking temperature.

Use:

1. Moderate-low heat to melt the fat and blend in the flour.

2. No heat when blending in the hot liquid.

3. Moderate-low heat to bring the sauce to a boil.

4. Simmering heat for additional cooking. (Or place sauce in a double boiler over simmering water.)

To thin sauces or gravies, add hot stock, milk, cream, or any other liquid required, and stir until blended. To thicken sauces, use one of these methods:

1. Reduce the liquid by cooking sauce more rapidly.

2. Add an egg yolk. Blend yolk with a few tablespoons of sauce away from heat. Add this slowly to the sauce as you stir. Do not allow sauce to boil or it will curdle. To keep it warm, place it in a double boiler over very shallow warm water.

3. Use flour. Mix a little flour smoothly with a minimum of cold water or other liquid, whisk slowly into hot sauce, and simmer a few minutes. If sauce lumps, strain it.

4. Use cornflour. Where a glazed sauce is desirable, blend it (1 teaspoon of cornflour about equals 1 tablespoon of flour) into a little cold liquid and stir into hot sauce. Cook several minutes.

For an acceptable gravy, blend a scant 2 tablespoons of flour into 2 tablespoons of melted butter or other fat. Whisk in 1 cup of hot unsalted vegetable liquor, $1\frac{1}{2}$ teaspoons of meat extract, a dash of Worcester Sauce, a pinch of thyme, and a sprinkling of pepper. Bring gravy to a boil, correct the seasoning, and simmer it 5 to 10 minutes.

⅍ ABOUT SALAD DRESSINGS

A fine salad dressing has a magic touch. It can tranform even plain Cinderella food. To be good, it should be well balanced, with a pleasing proportion of a good oil to a good vinegar. Such a dressing is French dressing. While garlic is used in the seasoning, it need not speak out loud, but can whisper delicately if you prefer. Introduce it in any of these ways. Decide which you prefer.

1. For a suspicion of garlic, rub the inside of a bowl, preferably wooden, with a split peeled clove. Discard what left.

2. For more flavour, place salt in the bowl and rub the peeled clove into it until it is mashed and disintegrates. Remove any shreds.

3. Or use a *chapon*—a small piece of toast or hard-crusted bread rubbed over with a garlic clove. Drop it into the bowl, dress the salad, and remove the *chapon* before serving. You may omit the garlic and still have a good dressing, but the salad will be a little like an unkissed bride.

The basic French dressing may be altered to fit the food it dresses by the addition of sugar, paprika, cayenne Tabasco, mustard, etc., and by using chopped fresh herbs, such as tarragon, chives, parsley, dill, chervil, basil, and oregano. A pinch of dried herb will do if fresh herbs are not available. The French dressing becomes Vinaigrette Sauce when mustard, herbs, and capers are included. It may be used for warm as well as cold salads.

⅍ FRENCH DRESSING

1 *small peeled garlic clove*	¼ *teaspoon salt*
3 *tablespoons good olive oil*	*Several grindings black*
1 *to* 1½ *tablespoons mild*	*pepper*
wine vinegar	

This amount of dressing may be sufficient for 1 medium-sized head of lettuce or the equivalent of other greens. Greens differ

160

so much in size, compactness, and texture, that it is hard to give exact quantities. Get a good French olive oil if possible. A mild red or rosé wine vinegar may be used. Lemon juice may replace part or all of the vinegar. Oil and vinegar are best applied to green salads, oil and vinegar separately. You may wish to prepare the dressing beforehand. Place the ingredients—except the garlic with which the bowl is rubbed —in a small jar and shake briskly. Immediately before using, shake it again. If the dressing is for other than green salads, add the garlic, crushed, to the jar and strain the dressing before using.

Besides these in this section, other salad dressings can be found elsewhere in the book (see Index) with the dishes they embellish.

✂ BÉCHAMEL SAUCE

MAKES 1 CUP · 15 TO 20 MINUTES

2 *tablespoons butter*	¼ *teaspoon salt*
1 *tablespoon chopped onion*	⅛ *teaspoon white pepper*
2 *tablespoons flour*	*Pinch nutmeg*
1 *cup hot milk (or ½ cup milk and ½ cup veal, chicken, or fish stock)*	

1. Melt butter in top of double boiler directly over low heat. Add onion and cook without browning 5 minutes.
2. Stir in flour and blend with wire whisk until smooth. Add liquid away from heat, stirring with whisk. Return to heat and whisk until mixture comes to a boil. Add seasoning. Place sauce over hot water and let it cook slowly 10 to 15 minutes. Strain if desired.
3. Serve sauce hot or use with dish as directed in recipe.

161

This is the common white sauce. For curried white sauce, add 1 teaspoon of curry or more, to taste, along with the flour, and proceed with the recipe. Add 1 teaspoon of lemon juice with the seasoning.

₩ VELOUTÉ SAUCE

Prepare in same way as Béchamel, using 1 cup all-veal or all-chicken stock and no milk. You've probably made this sauce as part of meat, fish, and vegetable dishes.

₩ MORNAY SAUCE

Make Béchamel Sauce. Stir into hot sauce 2 tablespoons of heavy cream and 2 tablespoons each of grated Parmesan and Gruyère (Swiss) cheese. Beat sauce well until cheese melts. Remove from heat and stir in 2 tablespoons of butter. Use with artichokes, poached fish, eggs.

₩ AURORE SAUCE

Cook a half cup each of Béchamel and Tomato Sauces over moderately low heat 5 minutes. Remove sauce from heat and stir in 1 tablespoon of butter. Fine with eggs, poached fish, croquettes.

₩ BROWN OR ESPAGNOLE SAUCE

Follow recipe for Béchamel Sauce, substituting for the liquid 1 cup of beef bouillon—fresh, tinned, or made with 1 cup of boiling water and 1 beef cube. Cook sauce without onion and let flour brown. Add to seasonings a piece of bay leaf, a sprig of parsley, and a pinch each of thyme and tarragon.

⑊ BASIC TOMATO SAUCE

MAKES 2½ CUPS · 2¼ HOURS

1 *small onion*	2 *pinches dried thyme,*
1 *small carrot*	*powdered with fingers*
1 *rib celery (no leaves)*	*Pinch dried basil*
1 *tin Italian peeled*	1 *to* 1½ *teaspoons salt*
tomatoes with or without	⅛ *teaspoon pepper*
basil	2 *sprigs parsley*
1 *small bay leaf*	1 *tablespoon olive oil or any*
	bland oil (optional)

1. Mince onion, carrot and celery.
2. Place them with all other ingredients, except oil, in an enamel-lined saucepan if you have one. Bring to boil, cover, and let boil gently over low heat 1 hour.
3. Mash tomatoes with the back of a fork or spoon. Keep them partially uncovered and continue to cook 30 minutes.
4. Add oil, keep uncovered, raise heat slightly, and cook 30 minutes more. Stir once or twice. Most of liquid should have evaporated.
5. Press sauce through food mill. Make sure every bit of tomato pulp and vegetable is pressed through. Sauce will be thick and creamy. Warm up if desired for immediate use, or refrigerate. It will keep several days.

This sauce may be used as it is over spaghetti. If a sharper flavour is wanted, sauté 2 tablespoons of chopped onion and 1 chopped garlic clove in 1 tablespoon of butter or oil 3 or 4 minutes. Add sauce and simmer 5 to 10 minutes. If a thinner sauce is needed, dilute with a small amount of chicken stock. Fresh tomatoes, 2 to 2½ pounds of plum tomatoes, may be substituted for tinned ones.

⅍ SAUCE FOR PAN-GRILLED STEAK

MAKES ABOUT ¾ CUP · 2 MINUTES

5 *tablespoons cognac or brandy*	1 *tablespoon prepared mustard*
5 *tablespoons Worcester Sauce*	

1. Combine brandy, Worcester Sauce, and mustard. Pour into a jar and shake well. Cover. You may use it at once or store it for future use; it will keep several months unrefrigerated.
2. When ready to use, shake sauce thoroughly. Add 3 tablespoons of melted butter to every scant 2 tablespoons of sauce.
3. When steak has been cooked on both sides, remove it to a hot platter. Pour off any fat in pan, but do not scrape pan. Pour mixed sauce into pan, and scrape and stir over high flame 1 minute. Spoon over steak.

⅍ FRENCH MAYONNAISE

MAKES ABOUT 1¼ CUPS · 10 MINUTES

1 *raw egg yolk*	¼ *teaspoon sugar (optional)*
1 *tablespoon wine vinegar*	1 *cup bland vegetable oil or*
1 *tablespoon lemon juice*	¾ *cup vegetable oil and ¼*
½ *teaspoon salt*	*cup good quality olive oil*
⅛ *teaspoon white pepper*	1½ *teaspoons boiling water*
⅛ *teaspoon dry mustard*	

1. Place all ingredients, except oil and water, into a bowl. Stir vigorously until smooth, about 1 minute.
2. Use electric or hand egg beater. Begin with ¼ teaspoon of oil; beat it into egg mixture thoroughly and constantly. Increase amounts of oil a little at a time; add in same way, beating

constantly, until all oil has been used or sauce is as thick as desired. Beat in boiling water. Allow 6 to 8 minutes for the making of the sauce.

This mayonnaise is both very simple to make and very good. You will have absolutely no difficulty with it if you beat in a little oil at a time and beat constantly. For garlic mayonnaise, drop in a garlic clove speared with a toothpick for easy removal. Keep it there until the degree of garlic flavour pleases you. Seasoned thus, the mayonnaise makes a fine dunk for raw vegetables.

GLOUCESTER SAUCE

Combine 1 cup of mayonnaise, $\frac{1}{4}$ cup of sour cream, the juice of half a lemon, $\frac{1}{2}$ teaspoon of chopped fennel leaves, and $\frac{1}{2}$ teaspoon of Worcester Sauce. Try this on cold meats.

CREAMY SALAD DRESSING

MAKES ABOUT $\frac{3}{4}$ CUP · 5 MINUTES

4 *tablespoons oil*	$\frac{3}{4}$ *teaspoon salt*
4 *tablespoons heavy cream*	*Pepper to taste*
3 *tablespoons wine vinegar*	
$\frac{1}{2}$ *teaspoon prepared mustard*	

1. Mix first 4 ingredients in an electric mixer or with a hand egg beater. Sauce should be quite thick.
2. Add salt and pepper to taste.

A very good sauce, easily made, and good with cold meats and fish as well as vegetables.

165

⅍ CREAMY SALAD DRESSING WITH KETCHUP

MAKES ⅓ CUP · 5 MINUTES

3 *tablespoons heavy cream*	1 *teaspoon sugar*
1 *teaspoon lemon juice*	½ *teaspoon salt*
2 *teaspoons wine vinegar*	⅛ *teaspoon white pepper*
4 *teaspoons tomato ketchup*	1 *teaspoon finely-grated onion*

1. Beat cream until very thick, but not as stiff as whipped cream.
2. Combine lemon juice, vinegar, ketchup, sugar, salt, pepper, and grated onion.
3. Add cream gradually and mix in well.

Good with wedges of iceberg lettuce.

⅍ ENGLISH SALAD DRESSING

MAKES 1 CUP · 10 MINUTES

2 *teaspoons prepared mustard*	½ *cup milk*
2 *teaspoons sugar*	¼ *cup mild vinegar*
½ *teaspoon salt*	*Pinch cayenne*
¼ *cup salad oil*	

1. Blend mustard, sugar, and salt.
2. Add oil, a few drops at a time, stirring constantly.
3. Add milk and then vinegar in same way as oil.
4. Season with cayenne. Keep refrigerated.

A fine dressing to use with greens, vegetables, and even meats.

166

DESSERTS: MOSTLY FRUITS AND PUDDINGS, WITH APPROPRIATE SAUCES

Ӿ　　Ӿ　　Ӿ　　Ӿ　　Ӿ　　Ӿ　　Ӿ　　Ӿ

T HE preponderance of simple fruit desserts and puddings in this section is part of the plan of this book. No one has, as far as I know, discovered a method of baking cakes or pie crusts on the top of the stove. And the desserts described herein are tasty and attractive without being too heavy in calories.

Nothing can match the satisfying, elegant simplicity of a bowl of fresh perfect fruit served with a platter of fine cheeses. Our fruit is unfortunately often sold partially ripe. Avoid the disappointment of biting into green fruit by giving it a chance to ripen in the kitchen. Keep the fruit in a paper bag or in a bowl at room temperature, away from the hot sun, for two or three days. Watch it; it sometimes rots rather than ripens. Whether ripe or not, select fruit carefully. Look out for bruises and hidden soft spots.

Today's good food stores are stocked with more and more cheeses. Get acquainted with unfamiliar ones; try them with fruit. You will find you prefer some combinations over others. Cheese seems to taste better when it is cut in slabs or cubes rather than in thin slices. Give chilled cheese a chance to soften outside the refrigerator; you'll be surprised at the difference in taste.

The puddings are nothing without their sauces. You won't find many of the sauces excessively rich. A spoonful or two of sauce is enough to embellish a serving.

✺ FRUIT FLAVOURED WITH LIQUEURS

Vary the taste of fruits and berries with a little liqueur or brandy. Kirsch, especially, with its bitter almond–cherry taste, is perfect with certain fruits. Triple Sec, Cointreau, and Grand Marnier, all orange-flavoured are also fruit enhancers. Brandy or cognac does something for almost every fruit. Rum and port, while not liqueurs, are also well suited to fruits. Serve fruits separately or in a macédoine. Fresh fruit is best, but frozen or tinned fruit may be used instead. The following is a list of liqueurs with the fruits they complement:

KIRSCH: pineapple, strawberries, apricots, cherries, peaches, nectarines, oranges.

COINTREAU OR GRAND MARNIER: orange, grapefruit, pineapple, and any other fruit that will combine happily with the orange flavour.

BRANDY: apricots, apples, bananas, and practically all other fruits.

RUM: apples, bananas, apricots, oranges, strawberries.

PORT: melon, cantaloupe, pineapple, strawberries.

TRY THESE COMBINATIONS:

strawberries and apricots with rum, kirsch, or brandy
strawberries and bananas with brandy
raspberries and peaches with kirsch or brandy
raspberries, strawberries, and peaches with kirsch or brandy
pineapple, grapefruit, and orange with Cointreau or Grand
    Marnier

pineapple, oranges, and strawberries with rum, kirsch, or Cointreau

melon, pineapple, and strawberries with port

dates, oranges, bananas, strawberries, and pineapple with rum

HOW TO USE LIQUEURS WITH FRUITS

FRESH FRUIT

1. Prepare a sugar syrup: boil together for 15 minutes 1 cup of water, 1 cup sugar, and ⅛ teaspoon of salt. Remove from heat and add ¼ teaspoon of vanilla extract. Chill.

2. Boil 10 minutes orange and lemon peel (coloured part only), cut julienne. Strain and chill.

3. Add enough sugar syrup to half cover the peeled, sliced, or diced fruit.

4. Begin with 1 tablespoon of liqueur or brandy, and mix well into fruit and syrup. Taste. Add a little more if you like. Throw in a few strips of prepared peel if the flavour fits. Chill 1 hour or until very cold.

5. Serve in glass dishes with just a little syrup.

TINNED FRUIT

Use tinned syrup in place of prepared syrup. Proceed as with fresh fruit.

FROZEN FRUIT OR BERRIES

After thawing, stir in liqueur and serve. Add no extra syrup.

FRESH BERRIES

1. Sprinkle plenty of powdered sugar over whole washed berries. (Slice large strawberries.) Let them steep about 2 to 3 hours or long enough for them to make their own syrup.

2. When mixing large amounts of sugared berries with other fruits, use berry syrup and add a tiny amount of other fruit syrup, just enough to moisten fruit. Stir in liqueur. Chill very well.

⅍ MORE WAYS WITH FRUIT

1. Purée drained tinned apricots. Combine with stiffly beaten sweetened egg white (2 tablespoons of sugar to 1 egg white) and some whipped cream. Sprinkle with a little kirsch or brandy.

2. Purée thawed frozen strawberries. Mix with melon cubes. Add sugar if necessary. Drizzle in a little port, and chill.

3. Use pistachio ice cream, or vanilla ice cream topped with chopped toasted pistachios. Top with minced, sugared fresh pineapple or drained, crushed tinned pineapple. Sprinkle with a little port. (Prepare fresh pineapple for use by dousing cored slices with powdered sugar and letting them stand 2 to 3 hours.)

4. Cover pineapple sherbet with sliced, sugared fresh strawberries and their syrup, or with thawed frozen strawberries.

5. Serve sliced peaches, bananas, apricots, or strawberries with sour cream and powdered sugar.

6. Stuff a ripe honeydew melon. Cut out a wedge large enough to enable you to remove the seeds. Scoop out the flesh and dice it. Mix it with raspberries and diced Bartlett pears, peaches, and bananas. Purée thawed frozen strawberries and mix with other fruit. Add sugar if necessary and a little port. Replace wedge and chill melon until icy cold. Serve in slices or spoon into glass dishes.

7. Chill tinned greengages with their syrup. Add a few slivers of preserved ginger.

8. Moisten a quarter of a cup of plump raisins with 1 tablespoon of brandy. Let stand 1 to 2 hours. Mix into 1 cup of applesauce.

⅍ CHEESE AND FRUIT FOR DESSERT

SUGGESTED COMBINATIONS

Roquefort, gorgonzola, or bleu with apples, pears, bananas
Bel Paese with cherries, plums, grapes
Camembert with pears, melon, peaches

Swiss or French Gruyère with almost any fruit
Taleggio with pears, grapes
Cheddar (well aged) with apples
King Christian with apples, pears
Edam with apples
Ricotta, cottage cheese, or cream cheese with pineapple,
    oranges, grapes
Port du Salut, oka, chantelle with almost all fruits

Of course, any combination of cheese and fruit that pleases
your palate is good. This list does not name all the fine
cheeses. It is meant to serve as a guide towards discovering
your own combinations.

SUGGESTED BISCUITS OR BREADS TO
ACCOMPANY THE CHEESES

Water biscuits
Rye crackers
Unsalted plain soda crackers
Melba toast
French or Italian bread
Thinly-sliced pumpernickel

Crackers and biscuits are improved by being lightly toasted
and buttered. For a "Come after dinner" Party or an
after-theatre get-together, a platter or tray of assorted
cheeses, biscuits, and breads, a bowl of fruit, a pot of coffee,
and some cookies for non-cheese-eaters (Are there any?)
make an easy but always acceptable way to entertain.

171

⚜ AMBROSIA

SERVES 4 · PREPARATION 15 MINUTES
CHILLING 3 HOURS

2 *large navel oranges*	2 *tablespoons powdered sugar*
1 *tin sliced pineapple*	1 *cup shredded coconut* ·
(4 *slices*)	2 *bananas*

1. Peel oranges and divide them into sections. Skin each section. Try to keep them in as large pieces as possible. Save juice.
2. Drain pineapple slices, saving juice. Cut slices into chunks.
3. Combine orange juice, pineapple juice, sugar, and coconut. Slice bananas.
4. Arrange alternate layers of orange, pineapple, and banana in a glass bowl. Sprinkle each layer with a little of the coconut mixture. Chill well.
5. Serve ambrosia in well-chilled individual dishes. Pour over each portion some juice from the bottom of the bowl.

⚜ APRICOT-GLAZED APPLES

SERVES 6 · 1 HOUR

6 *large apples*	¾ *cup water*
4 *tablespoons raisins*	6 *tablespoons sugar*
2 or 3 *strips lemon peel*	*Pinch salt*
¾ *cup apricot jam or*	¼ *cup blanched almonds*
preserves	4 to 6 *tablespoons rum*

1. Plump up raisins by soaking them in hot water 1 minute. Squeeze them dry. Remove white part from lemon peel. Beginning at stem end, remove from each apple all but the last half-inch of core. Also pare the top inch of each apple.
2. Combine next 5 ingredients in a saucepan just large enough to enable each apple to rest on bottom, and cook over medium heat until blended. Lower heat. Place apples in pan; simmer

172

covered about 45 minutes; baste them often with syrup. Use an asbestos pad if necessary to keep heat at simmering point. If syrup is permitted to boil, apples will cook too fast and may burst. Sliver and toast almonds.

3. With a slotted spoon remove apples to a serving dish. Spoon a little syrup over them to make a glaze. Add rum to remaining syrup and pour into dish of apples. Sprinkle tops with nuts.

4. Serve apples at room temperature.

ꓤ RUM-GLAZED APPLES

SERVES 4 TO 6 · PREPARATION 30 MINUTES
CHILLING SEVERAL HOURS

4 *large apples*	1 *tablespoon cold water*
1 *cup water*	2 *or 3 drops red food colouring*
½ *cup sugar*	2 *or more tablespoons rum*
A 2-*inch piece vanilla bean or*	¼ *cup hazelnuts or filberts*
½ *teaspoon vanilla extract*	½ *pound large-curd cottage*
1 *teaspoon cornflour*	*cheese*

1. Boil water slowly with sugar and vanilla bean for 15 minutes. While syrup cooks, core and peel apples and slice them into eighths.

2. Blend cornflour with water and stir it into cooked syrup. Continue stirring until syrup comes to a boil, and cook slowly 2 minutes. Shake in food colouring and stir. Flavour with 2 tablespoons of rum, or more to taste. Add apples and cook slowly about 5 minutes or until they are soft but not mushy, basting frequently to glaze them. Remove apples and vanilla bean from syrup.

3. Reduce syrup over moderate heat to ½ cup. Add vanilla extract at this time if bean was not used. Return apples to syrup. Let them chill several hours or overnight.

4. Skin, chop, and toast nuts. For individual servings, place 1

heaped tablespoon of cheese in each dish. Surround with
several sections of apple. Drizzle a little syrup over the
cheese; sprinkle with nuts.

⊱ BRANDIED APPLE FRITTERS

SERVES 4 · 50 MINUTES

4 *medium-sized apples*	2 *tablespoons sugar*
4 *tablespoons brandy or rum*	1 *cup flour*
2 *tablespoons sugar*	1 *tablespoon melted butter or*
2 *eggs, separated*	*bland oil*
⅓ *cup milk*	*Fat for deep frying*
⅓ *cup water*	*Powdered sugar*
¼ *teaspoon salt*	

1. Dissolve sugar in brandy or rum. Core and peel apples. Slice
   them ½ inch thick into liquor. Let them steep at least 30
   minutes.
2. Combine egg yolks, milk, water, salt, and sugar. Beat well.
   Add flour and stir quickly with a few strokes until mixture is
   quite smooth. Stir in butter or oil.
3. Beat egg whites until stiff. Fold into batter.
4. Have ready a pan of deep, hot fat, about 360° F. Dip undrained apple slices into batter. Fry them until they are
   golden brown, 2 to 3 minutes. Drain them on absorbent
   paper. Sprinkle with powdered sugar.

⊱ FRENCH FRITTERS

SERVES 4 · 30 MINUTES

APRICOT SAUCE

4 *preserved kumquats (op-*	½ *cup water*
tional)	2 *tablespoons Cointreau or*
½ *cup apricot jam*	*Grand Marnier*

174

FRENCH FRITTER BATTER

1 *egg white*	*Oil for deep frying*
½ *cup water*	2 *eggs*
2 *tablespoons butter*	1 *teaspoon baking powder*
½ *cup flour*	

Icing sugar

To make APRICOT SAUCE: If you are using kumquats, slice them thinly and remove seeds. Blend jam and water in a small pan over low heat. Remove pan from heat. Add liqueur and stir. Add kumquats. Set aside sauce and keep it warm.

1. To make FRENCH FRITTERS, beat egg white until stiff and dry. Reserve.

2. Slowly bring water and butter to boil in a medium-sized saucepan. Add flour all at once. Stir over heat vigorously a few seconds with a wooden spoon until mixtures leaves sides of pan. Remove pan from heat.

3. Set oil to heat slowly in a deep pan.

4. Beat eggs one at a time into flour mixture with a wooden spoon. Beat about 2 minutes after each egg is added. Then finish beating with rotary hand beater until batter is smooth, about 2 minutes. Fold in baking powder and stiff egg white lightly and quickly.

5. Drop batter by teaspoonfuls into hot oil, about 350° F. Do not overcrowd fritters. Cook until they are delicately brown all over, about 30 seconds. Remove them with slotted spoon. Drain them on absorbent paper.

6. Dust fritters with sugar. Serve them at once with APRICOT SAUCE.

These are delightfully light fritters which never fail. If an inexpensive impressive dessert is wanted, this is it. It is good, too, without the sauce.

175

❧ AVOCADO PEAR IN KIRSCH

SERVES 4 · PREPARATION 10 MINUTES
CHILLING SEVERAL HOURS

1½ *lemons*　　　　　　　　　*Pinch nutmeg*
2 *ripe avocado pears*　　　 2 *tablespoons kirsch*
2 *to 3 tablespoons castor*
　sugar

1. Cut 1 lemon in half. Reserve. Squeeze juice from remaining lemon half.

2. Cut 1 avocado pear in half. Remove stone. Rub immediately with cut lemon, squeezing some juice over each half. Cut out pulp with a knife or scoop it out carefully with a teaspoon. Dice it quickly and mix with 1 teaspoon lemon juice. Follow the same procedure with the second avocado pear.

3. Sprinkle avocado pulp with sugar and nutmeg. Moisten with kirsch. Gently stir to blend seasoning and flavouring. It may need a little more lemon juice or sugar; it should be tartish, neither sweet nor very tart.

4. Cover and chill several hours. Serve very cold in a glass dish.

A refreshing light dessert very good as is or with a lemon-flavoured cookie.

❧ CHERRIES JUBILEE

SERVES 4 TO 6
METHOD 1 · 35 MINUTES

1 *pound Bing cherries*　　　*Cornflour*
1 *cup water*　　　　　　　 ¼ *cup or more kirsch*
½ *cup sugar*　　　　　　　 1 *quart vanilla ice cream*

1. Wash, drain well, and stone cherries.

2. Boil water and sugar 10 minutes over medium-low heat. Add cherries and cook about 5 minutes until they are soft but still smooth. Strain into a small heat-proof serving dish if you have one.

3. Reduce syrup over medium heat, cooking it about 5 minutes. Measure it. Allow 1 tablespoon of cornflour blended with $1\frac{1}{2}$ tablespoons of cold water to each cup of syrup. Lower heat. Add cornflour mixture to syrup and stir until it boils. Cook 2 minutes to clear it. Return cherries to syrup, and heat.

4. Heat kirsch in a small pan or over a candle burner. Arrange ice cream on individual dessert plates. At table pour kirsch over hot cherries in serving dish. Ignite with a lighted match. Spoon syrup over cherries when flame begins to die down. Serve over ice cream.

METHOD 2 · 20 MINUTES

1 *pound tinned stoned Bing cherries*

Drain syrup well from tinned cherries. Omit Step 2. Proceed with Step 3 and Step 4.

METHOD 3 · 25 MINUTES

1 *pound Bing cherries*   5 *tablespoons water*
1 *jar redcurrant jelly*, 10 or
   12 *ounces*

1. Wash, drain well, and stone cherries.

2. Combine jelly and water in a pan and melt over medium-low heat. Add cherries; stir until heated through and tender, with skins still smooth.

3. Proceed now with Step 4.

⅍ FRUIT COMPÔTE

SERVES 8 TO 10 · PREPARATION 35 TO 40 MINUTES
CHILLING 2 TO 3 HOURS

1 *Comice pear*	½ *pound seedless grapes*
½ *cup water*	1 *cup fresh or drained tinned*
½ *cup sauterne wine*	*pineapple cubes*
¾ *cup sugar*	2 *oranges*
A *2-inch piece vanilla bean or*	1 *apple*
½ *teaspoon vanilla extract*	2 *peaches*
A *1-inch piece of cinnamon*	1 *pint strawberries*
stick	3 *tablespoons icing sugar*
2 *small strips lemon peel*	

1. Peel, halve, and core pear. Combine water, wine, sugar, vanilla bean, cinnamon, lemon peel, and pear halves. Cook these slowly until pear is tender but firm. Remove pear, vanilla bean, and cinnamon.

2. Boil down syrup until it is reduced by half. Strain it into a large dish. Add vanilla extract if bean was not used.

3. While syrup cooks, remove stems from grapes, cube pineapple, and separate oranges into sections, removing membrane. Add the first two to the hot strained liquid. Reserve oranges. Peel and dice apple; peel and slice peaches; and add these. Turn fruit gently to moisten. Cover. When cool, add orange sections with their juice and cubed cooked pear. Cover and chill until icy cold.

4. Hull strawberries and slice them into a separate dish. Sprinkle them with sugar. Chill.

5. A few minutes before serving, combine fruits and syrups in a large glass bowl. Serve a spoonful or two of syrup with each portion.

Cut fruit into bite-sized pieces, as there is nothing so unappealing as mushy fruit. For 4 to 5 servings, use ⅓ cup of water, ½ cup of wine, ½ cup of sugar, a small pear, quartered, ¼ pound of grapes, 1 orange, half an apple, 1 peach, ½ pint of strawberries, and 2 tablespoons of powdered sugar. Don't add cooked pear to compôte; save it for solo supping.

⅍ ORANGE COMPÔTE

SERVES 8 · PREPARATION 1 HOUR
CHILLING OVERNIGHT

4 *very large navel oranges*	2 *to 3 drops red food colouring*
1⅓ *cups sugar*	2 *or more tablespoons Grand*
⅛ *teaspoon salt*	*Marnier, kirsch, or brandy*
2 *cups water*	(*optional*)

1. Cut peel from orange with a knife. Scrape off with tip of a teaspoon any white underskin that adheres. Cut away underskin from peeled oranges. Be careful not to pierce membrane protecting orange sections. Separate each orange into halves. Cut peel into narrow short, even strips.

2. Place peel in cold water to cover. Bring to boil over moderate heat; then drain. Repeat this process 4 more times. Reserve drained peel.

3. Add sugar and salt to 2 cups of water and boil 15 minutes over moderate heat. Add orange halves and food colouring. Bring to boil. Cook slowly 5 minutes. Remove fruit to serving bowl. Cook syrup quickly to reduce it by half.

4. Add peel to oranges and pour hot syrup over them. Add liqueur or brandy if desired. Chill compôte thoroughly. Serve some of the peel and juice with each orange half.

This dessert takes time to make but is definitely worth it. You may have a different way of removing the white pith from oranges; I have found the above method the speediest. The

179

peel may be altogether omitted if you wish. Or if you like a slight bitter taste, add the uncooked orange peel to the water at the same time as the sugar and salt. Pre-cooking the peel removes some of the bitterness. I have prepared these oranges both ways and found the difference in taste very slight.

✢ CARDINAL PEACHES

SERVES 6 · PREPARATION 30 TO 35 MINUTES
CHILLING 2 HOURS

6 *ripe, firm peaches*	1 *jar raspberry jelly*
½ *cup sugar*	2 *tablespoons water*
1 *cup water*	1 *tablespoon or more kirsch*
A 2-*inch piece vanilla bean or*	½ *cup blanched almonds*
¼ *teaspoon vanilla extract*	

1. Boil sugar, water, and vanilla bean slowly 15 minutes.
2. Meanwhile peel, halve, and stone peaches. Poach them in the simmering syrup about 15 minutes or until they are soft but still firm. Remove bean. Add extract now if bean was not used. Let fruit cool in syrup. Chill.
3. Heat jelly slowly with water until it is dissolved. Strain. Add kirsch to taste. Cool.
4. Sliver and toast almonds.
5. Serve 2 well-drained peach halves in a glass dish for each serving. Partially cover with raspberry sauce. Sprinkle with almond slivers.

You may use RASPBERRY SAUCE instead of above sauce made with jelly. Or bottled Melba Sauce may be purchased. Tinned peaches may be used when fresh ones are out of season. Just add vanilla extract to the fruit and syrup, and chill. Proceed with Steps 3, 4, and 5.

❧ Variation · MÉLANGE OF RASPBERRIES AND PEACHES

SERVES 8 · PREPARATION 5 MINUTES
THAWING 4 TO 5 HOURS

One 10-ounce packet frozen raspberries	*Two 12-ounce packets frozen peaches' or one 20-ounce tin sliced peaches*

Place drained tinned peaches or unthawed frozen peaches in a serving bowl. Top with frozen raspberries and let them thaw out over peaches. Serve icy cold.

This simple but excellent combination of flavours is very good with vanilla ice cream. It makes a fine dessert for emergencies. In fact it is almost like PEACH MELBA.

❧ TINNED PEACHES IN WINE

SERVES 4 · PREPARATION 15 TO 20 MINUTES
CHILLING SEVERAL HOURS

1 tin (about 1 pound) peach slices or halves	*3 tablespoons sugar*
2 or 3 strips lemon peel	*A 2-inch piece vanilla bean or ½ teaspoon vanilla extract*
½ cup peach syrup	*2 or 3 tablespoons brandy or cognac*
½ cup white wine or port	

1. Strain syrup from peaches into a dish. Remove white part from lemon peel.
2. Combine syrup, wine, sugar, vanilla bean, and lemon peel. Bring to a boil; cook slowly 10 to 15 minutes until syrup thickens and reduces somewhat. Discard peel and bean.
3. Cool syrup. Add brandy or cognac, vanilla extract, if bean was not used, and drained peaches.
4. Chill several hours.

Serve as it is or with a plain cookie.

⅊ **Variation**

For TINNED PEARS IN SAUTERNE, substitute Bartlett pears. Use sauterne for the wine. Include a 1-inch piece of cinnamon stick in Step 2 and discard along with peel and bean.

⅊ **PEARS IN RUM SYRUP**

SERVES 4 · PREPARATION 40 MINUTES
CHILLING 2 HOURS

1 *cup water*	4 *Comice pears*
½ *cup sugar*	*Cornflour*
A 2-inch piece vanilla bean or	1 *or* 2 *drops red food colouring*
½ *teaspoon vanilla extract*	1 *or* 2 *tablespoons rum*

1. Boil slowly water, sugar, and vanilla bean for 15 minutes.
2. Peel, halve, and core pears. Add them to syrup and cook until tender but still firm, about 15 to 20 minutes. Remove pears and vanilla bean.
3. Measure syrup. Dissolve 1 teaspoon of cornflour in 1 tablespoon of cold water for each ½ cup of syrup. Stir into syrup. Let it come to a boil, stirring all the time until syrup is thick and clear. Add vanilla extract now if bean was not used. Add enough colouring to make syrup pink.
4. Begin with 1 tablespoon of rum, and flavour syrup to taste. Let pears cool in syrup. Refrigerate.
5. Serve with a little syrup spooned over the pear halves.

⅊ **PEACH MELBA**

SERVES 4 · PREPARATION 25 TO 30 MINUTES
CHILLING SEVERAL HOURS

4 *large fresh peaches*	1 *cup sugar*
½ *cup white wine*	*A 2-inch piece vanilla bean or*
½ *cup water*	½ *teaspoon vanilla extract*

182

RASPBERRY SAUCE

1 *cup tinned or frozen*	$\frac{1}{2}$ *teaspoon cornflour*
raspberries	1 *tablespoon water*
$\frac{1}{4}$ *cup sugar*	2 *to 4 drops red food colouring*
Piece vanilla bean or $\frac{1}{4}$	
teaspoon vanilla extract	
1$\frac{1}{2}$ *pints vanilla ice cream*	$\frac{1}{4}$ *cup blanched almonds*
$\frac{1}{2}$ *cup heavy cream, whipped*	
(*optional*)	

1. Drop peaches into a bowl of boiling water for 1 minute. Skin peaches; halve and stone them.

2. Bring wine, water, sugar, and vanilla bean to a boil. Cook peach halves gently in the syrup about 6 minutes. Peaches should still be firm though tender. Remove vanilla bean. If bean was not used, add extract now. Cool fruit in syrup and refrigerate.

3. To make RASPBERRY SAUCE, sieve raspberries into small saucepan. Add sugar and vanilla bean (use same piece) and cook slowly 5 minutes. Blend cornflour with water. Stir into raspberry syrup. Boil up and cook for 2 minutes. Remove vanilla bean. Add extract now if bean was not used. Shake in food colouring and stir well to mix. Cool sauce and refrigerate. Sliver and toast almonds.

4. To serve, place a ball of ice cream in an individual serving dish with a drained peach half on each side. Pour over raspberry sauce. Top with whipped cream (optional). Sprinkle with 1 tablespoon of slivered almonds.

Peaches, sauce, and almonds can all be prepared a day ahead, which makes this delicious dessert ideal to serve. The whipped cream is not essential to its enjoyment. When fresh peaches are out of season, drained tinned peaches will do. Let them steep 15 minutes or so in a little brandy. In an emergency, use QUICK RASPBERRY SAUCE.

⚓ QUICK RASPBERRY SAUCE

MAKES 1 CUP · 5 MINUTES

1 *cup raspberry jam or jelly*   2 *tablespoons water*

1. Add water to jam or jelly. Heat slowly just long enough to blend.
2. Strain. Cool.

An emergency sauce for ice cream, bread, and cake pudding; a fine glaze for one-crust cherry pies.

⚓ PRUNES AND KUMQUATS AU COGNAC

SERVES 10 TO 12 · PREPARATION 25 MINUTES
CHILLING 24 TO 48 HOURS

1 *piece lemon peel, 1 inch*   *A 2-inch piece cinnamon stick*
  square   1 *pound tenderized prunes*
1 *jar preserved kumquats (10*   3 *tablespoons light raisins*
  or 12 ounces, about 15   2 *tablespoons cognac or*
  kumquats)   *brandy*
⅓ *cup sugar*
A 2-inch piece vanilla bean or
  ½ *teaspoon vanilla extract*

1. Cut lemon peel into tiny strips. Pour off kumquat syrup into a measuring cup. Add enough water to make 2 cups of liquid. Place liquid in a pan with sugar, vanilla bean, cinnamon stick, lemon peel, prunes, and raisins. Bring to a boil and cook over moderate heat 15 minutes.
2. Remove cinnamon stick and vanilla bean. Add vanilla extract now if bean was not used. Pour compôte with syrup into a dish large enough so that the fruit will not be crowded; the prunes will swell somewhat. Add whole kumquats. Stir in cognac or brandy and cover. Refrigerate when cool.
3. Use after 24 hours.

This is better if it stands 2 days before using.

❧ PRUNE WHIP

SERVES 8 · PREPARATION 10 MINUTES
CHILLING 2 HOURS

1 *pint puréed prunes (2 tins baby food)*
Grated rind of 1 *lemon*
1 *tablespoon lemon juice*

1 *tablespoon frozen concentrated orange juice*
2 *egg whites*

1. Empty prunes into a bowl. Grate in lemon rind. Add lemon juice and orange juice. Mix well.
2. Whip egg whites until they are stiff and dry. Fold them into prunes. Chill well.
3. Serve the dessert chilled as is or with a tablespoon or two of cream per serving.

   A simple, quickly made dessert, good for emergencies, and providing a good use for extra egg whites.

❧ STRAWBERRIES IN LIQUEUR

SERVES 6 · PREPARATION 15 MINUTES
STEEPING 1 HOUR
CHILLING 3 TO 4 HOURS

1 *quart strawberries*
½ *cup powdered sugar*
1 *tablespoon Cointreau*
1 *tablespoon kirsch*

2 *tablespoons brandy or cognac*
6 *sponge cake slices or 6 sponge cup cakes*

1. Wash, hull, and drain berries. Slice them.
2. Sprinkle sugar over them, and gently mix.
3. Pour liqueurs over strawberries and carefully mix. Cover.
4. Let berries stand at room temperature 1 hour. Then refrigerate. Chill 3 or 4 hours.
5. Serve as it is or over slices of sponge cake or in slightly scooped-out sponge cup cakes.

If you are not counting calories, heavy cream whipped stiff and combined with the berries is heavenly. But pour off much of the syrup before folding in the whipped cream; an excess of syrup will dilute the cream.

⅍ ALMOND SOUFFLÉ PUDDING

SERVES 4 · 1¼ HOURS

2 *tablespoons flour, sifted after measuring*	½ *cup milk*
	2 *tablespoons sugar*
3 *tablespoons blanched almonds*	2 *teaspoons kirsch (optional)*
	2 *egg yolks*
2 *tablespoons butter*	3 *egg whites*

BLACK RASPBERRY SAUCE

½ *cup black raspberry jelly*   1 *tablespoon port*
2 *tablespoons orange juice*

1. Butter well the inside of a soufflé dish. Dust it lightly with sugar. Tie a double band of greased paper round outside of dish so that it stands 2 or 3 inches above the rim of dish. Have ready a steamer, or a large pot with a rack, and enough boiling water to come no more than half-way up the side of the mould.

2. Sift flour. Chop almonds and toast them lightly.

3. Melt butter in a saucepan over low heat. Stir in flour. Add milk and stir constantly until mixture thickens, boils, and then leaves sides of pan. Cool 1 minute.

4. Mix in sugar, almonds, and flavouring.

5. Beat in yolks, one at a time, thoroughly.

6. Beat whites until very stiff and fold in lightly.

7. Turn mixture into prepared soufflé dish. Cover with greased paper. Set on rack. Cover steamer tightly. Turn heat very low and let water boil gently 45 minutes. Remove soufflé dish from water. Cool it 2 minutes. Remove paper cover and band. Slip

186

a knife carefully round the edges and loosen soufflé. Turn it out slowly on to a plate. Serve it immediately with BLACK RASPBERRY SAUCE.

8. To make BLACK RASPBERRY SAUCE, combine ingredients listed in a small saucepan. Heat them slowly until jelly is melted. Serve sauce warm or at room temperature.

A light and delicate steamed soufflé. An equal quantity of chopped candied cherries which have been steeped in a tablespoon of kirsch for 3 or 4 hours may be used in place of the almonds.

✄ CHESTNUT PUDDING

SERVES 4 TO 6 · 2 TO 2½ HOURS

12 *chestnuts*	3 *egg yolks*
Milk	6 *tablespoons sugar*
3 *tablespoons butter, at room*	*Grated rind of 1 lemon*
temperature	¼ *teaspoon cinnamon*
¼ *cup candied fruit peel, any*	½ *teaspoon cornflour*
mixture	3 *egg whites*
¼ *cup raisins*	

1. Butter a 7½- or 8-inch ring mould. Have ready a steamer or a large pot with a rack, and enough boiling water to come halfway up sides of mould.

2. Cover chestnuts with boiling water and boil them 7 or 8 minutes. Remove peel and inner skin.

3. Place chestnuts in milk to cover in the top of a double boiler over simmering water. Cook them until they are very soft. This takes a long time—at least an hour. Drain chestnuts well. Press them through a food mill or fine sieve.

4. Cream butter. Mince candied fruit fine. Soften raisins, if they are hard, in hot water; drain and dry them well. Beat egg

187

yolks and sugar together 5 minutes. Add butter, candied fruit peel, raisins, grated lemon rind, cinnamon, cornflour, and chestnut pulp.

5. Beat egg whites until very stiff and add them. Mix all lightly but thoroughly. Pour into prepared mould. Cover mould snugly with aluminium foil, and set it on rack in vigorously boiling water. Cover and let steam over low heat 35 to 40 minutes. Insert knife into pudding. If pudding is firm, remove mould from water. Allow pudding to cool 5 minutes. Slip knife around pudding to loosen and carefully invert it over a large plate.

6. Serve it warm with chilled COFFEE RUM SAUCE.

Pudding may be reheated over hot water, but it is better without reheating. To shorten cooking time, boil chestnuts directly over heat, in water in place of milk.

✂ COFFEE RUM SAUCE

MAKES 1 CUP · PREPARATION 40 MINUTES
CHILLING 3 HOURS

¾ cup water	Pinch salt
2 rounded teaspoons instant coffee	¼ cup milk
½ cup sugar	3 egg yolks
	3 tablespoons rum

1. Have ready about ¾ inch of simmering water in the bottom of a double boiler, over low heat.

2. Dissolve coffee in boiling water in a saucepan. Stir in sugar, salt, and hot milk.

3. Place egg yolks in the top of double boiler, away from heat. Whisk in coffee mixture, a little at a time.

4. Set top over simmering water, stirring with spoon continuously until sauce thickens and coats spoon, about 10 minutes. (Don't turn up heat to hasten cooking, or sauce will curdle.)

Remove from heat and pour all but ¼ cup of sauce into a bowl. Heat rum in a small pan. Turn off heat. Touch lighted match to rum. Let it burn about 10 or 15 seconds, or until half of rum is left; pour it immediately over sauce in pan. Combine both sauces.

5. Serve sauce warm or chilled; it is better chilled.

Chilling mellows the sauce and brings out the wonderful rum flavour. Chocolate and vanilla ice cream belong with this sauce.

⚜ COCONUT PUDDING, JIFFY RUM SAUCE

SERVES 4 · 1¼ HOURS

3 *ounces coconut cookies,*	2 *eggs*
store variety	¼ *cup sugar*
3 *tablespoons currants,*	*Grated rind and juice 1 orange*
washed	1 *tablespoon brandy or*
1 *cup milk*	*cognac*

JIFFY RUM SAUCE

1 *egg white*	3 *tablespoons milk*
3 *tablespoons sugar*	1 *tablespoon rum*
1 *egg yolk*	

1. Grease well the sides and bottom of a 1½-pint mould with a cover. (A 1-pound coffee tin makes a fine mould.) Dust the bottom lightly with sugar. Have ready a large pot with a trivet or rack in it. Fill it with boiling water that will come half-way up mould. Keep water at this level. If water drops much below, add more boiling water.

2. Soak cookies and currants in milk. Beat eggs well. Beat sugar into eggs gradually. Stir this into cookie-milk mixture and blend all together. Make sure cookies are dissolved. Blend in rind, juice, and brandy.

189

3. Pour mixture into mould and cover. Set mould on trivet with required amount of boiling water. Let water boil up a few seconds to produce steam. Cover pot, and simmer 1 hour.

4. Test pudding with knife for firmness. Pudding should be firm enough to keep its shape when it is removed from mould. If necessary, loosen it by running a knife around it. Invert it on a plate. Serve it warm with sauce.

5. To make JIFFY RUM SAUCE, beat egg white until stiff. Beat in sugar. Stir in unbeaten egg yolk and blend. Stir in milk and rum. Pour sauce over each serving.

An old-fashioned pleasant dessert that is easy to prepare and requires practically no attention. The sauce, as its name suggests, is whipped up in a jiffy. Add a little more sugar to the yolks if you like a very sweet sauce.

⚜ LADYFINGER PUDDING

SERVES 5 · 1½ HOURS

2 *to* 3 *tablespoons sugar for*
   sprinkling
2 *tablespoons raisins*
2 *eggs*
¼ *cup sugar*
Grated rind of 1 *lemon*

1 *cup milk*
8 *to* 12 *ladyfingers*
2 *or more tablespoons apricot*
   jam or orange marmalade
2 *tablespoons sherry*

1. Butter generously the insides of 5 custard cups, and sprinkle buttered surfaces with sugar. Set out a large steamer or a pot with cover and rack. Fill with hot water to reach halfway to two-thirds up sides of cups.

2. Steep raisins in a little hot water 2 minutes, and squeeze out water. Beat eggs 20 to 30 seconds with a hand beater. Add sugar and beat a few seconds. Grate in rind. Add milk and beat together to blend.

3. Split ladyfingers lengthwise in two. Place 1 teaspoon of raisins in bottom of each cup. Press a split ladyfinger half over raisins. Top with 1 teaspoon of jam or marmalade. Line sides of mould in 3 or 4 places, using 2 more split halves. If they crumble, pat them into place. Pour egg-milk mixture into cups ⅔ full. Cover snugly with aluminium foil.

4. Set cups on rack in pot. Bring water to boil. Reduce heat and cook very slowly 1 hour.

5. Remove cups from water. Let them stand a few moments. Invert them on to a dish.

6. Serve warm or cold. Pour 1 teaspoon of sherry over each pudping. If a sauce is desired, omit sherry and serve with APRICOT-ORANGE or SHERRY SAUCE.

A very easy pudding to prepare. Place it to cook and forget about it for 1 hour; it always comes out right, and tastes good, too. Try it with sliced sugared strawberries. If a single mould is preferred, use a 1½-pint mould and follow the same procedure. A few more ladyfingers and a bit more jam may be required.

APRICOT-ORANGE SAUCE

MAKES ¾ CUP · 5 MINUTES

½ cup apricot preserves or
   jam
¼ cup orange juice

2 *tablespoons rum or brandy*
   or 1 *tablespoon kirsch*

1. Combine preserves or jam with juice. Heat slowly, stirring until blended, about 2 minutes.

2. Remove from heat and stir in rum, brandy, or kirsch.

3. Serve sauce warm or chilled.

✄ SHERRY SAUCE

MAKES ⅔ CUP · 10 MINUTES

2 *tablespoons butter* 2 *tablespoons sugar*
½ *teaspoon flour* ⅛ *teaspoon salt*
¼ *cup sherry* 2 *egg yolks*

1. Melt butter in a small saucepan over medium-low hat. Blend in flour and stir until smooth.

2. Add wine, sugar, and salt. Stir and bring to boil. Remve from heat.

3. Beat egg yolks a few seconds. Add them slowly to wine nx-ture. Return to simmering heat and let sauce warm uj to simmering point only. Do not boil it, or it will curdle nd spoil. Remove sauce from heat. Serve it warm.

Try these sauces on ice cream, bread puddings, cake pd-dings.

✄ PARADISE PUDDING, APPLE-CRANBERRY SAUCE

SERVES 6 · 1¾ HOURS

2 *to* 3 *tablespoons sugar for* *Pinch salt*
sprinkling ⅛ *teaspoon cinnamon*
¼ *cup blanched almonds* 3 *tablespoons rum*
¼ *cup dried currants* ⅔ *cup matzo meal*
2 *eggs* 2 *large apples*
6 *tablespoons sugar* *Grated rind of* ½ *lemon*

APPLE-CRANBERRY SAUCE

1 *tin jellied cranberry sauce* 1 *tablespoon sugar*
  (7 *ounces*) *Grated rind of* ½ *orange*
3 *tablespoons apple juice.*

1. Grease the insides of 6 custard cups thoroughly with btter. Sprinkle sugar over butter surfaces. Set out a large steamr, or

192

a pot with a cover and rack. (A large plate can serve as a rack.) Fill steamer with hot water to reach halfway up cups.

2. Sliver almonds and toast them. Soak currants in hot water 1 minute and squeeze them dry.

3. Beat eggs very well. Add sugar, salt, and cinnamon, and beat them into eggs. Mix in rum. Add matzo, meal gradually; blend with mixture. Coarsely grate apple, finely grate lemon rind, add with almonds and currants. Mix all well.

4. Fill greased cups only ⅔ full. Cover cups snugly with double thickness of aluminium foil. Set them on to rack or plate. Bring water to rolling boil. Reduce heat, cover, and simmer 1½ hours.

5. Remove cups from water. Let them stand 2 or 3 minutes. Turn them out on to serving dish. Serve them warm with warm APPLE-CRANBERRY SAUCE.

6. To make APPLE-CRANBERRY SAUCE, combine Cranberry Sauce, apple juice, and sugar. Heat until Cranberry Sauce melts. Grate in orange rind.

❧ PECAN SPONGE PUDDING

SERVES 6 · 40 MINUTES

1½ teaspoons powdered cinnamon	2 tablespoons chopped pecans
½ cup finely ground or chopped pecans	5 eggs
	1 cup sugar

1. Grease 6 half-cup moulds. Fill a large deep pan with enough simmering water to come halfway up sides of moulds. Set a rack in the pan.

2. Add cinnamon to pecan meats. Chop very finely or grind in a nut grinder enough pecans to make ½ cup. Sieve them. Chop 2 tablespoons of nuts into small bits and reserve.

3. Beat eggs 1 minute with an electric beater or 2 minutes with a hand beater. Add sugar, 1 or 2 tablespoons at a time, beating thoroughly each time. Add ½ cup ground nuts and beat well again. Stir in reserved nuts.

4. Fill moulds ⅔ full with mixture. Cover them loosely with greased aluminium foil, allowing room for puddings to rise a little. Place moulds on rack, cover pan, and let steam in simmering water 17 to 20 minutes. Test with knife by inserting it into pudding. If it emerges dry, remove from water. Let cool 1 to 2 minutes. Turn puddings out over dish.

5. Serve them at room temperature with JIFFY RUM SAUCE.

As the name suggests, these turn out light and spongy. Quick to put together and quick to cook, they are well suited to finish off a summer luncheon or supper.

TIPSY TRIFLES

MAKES ABOUT 30 TO 35 BALLS · PREPARATION 30 MINUTES
STORE 24 HOURS

8 *ounces chocolate wafers*	*Pinch salt*
1 *cup icing sugar*	2 *tablespoons pancake syrup*
½ *cup chopped walnuts*	6 *tablespoons whisky*
½ *cup chopped pecans*	¼ *cup granulated sugar*

1. Crumble and sift wafers into a large bowl. There should be about 2 cups after sifting. Sift sugar on to crumbs.

2. Chop nuts into small bits, neither fine nor coarse. Add with salt to crumbs. Mix well with hand.

3. Combine syrup and whisky. Add slowly to crumb mixture with hand, pressing it together as you mix.

4. Place ¼ cup sugar on waxed paper. Shape mixture into walnut-sized balls and roll in sugar.

5. Store in waxed paper-lined tin box at least 24 hours to ripen. They will keep many days.

If mixture is too dry to shape, add a little more syrup. More liquor would make the trifles too strong and nibblers too weak.

ᕽᵉ COLD LEMON SOUFFLÉ, ORANGE DESSERT SAUCE

SERVES 4 OR 5 · PREPARATION 25 MINUTES
CHILLING $3\frac{1}{2}$ TO $4\frac{1}{2}$ HOURS

Grated rind of 1 lemon	*2 eggs*
Juice of 2 lemons	*2 egg yolks*
4 tablespoons cold water	*5 tablespoons sugar*
1 tablespoon plus 1 teaspoon unflavoured gelatine	*2 tablespoons whipped cream*

ORANGE DESSERT SAUCE

$\frac{1}{4}$ cup orange juice	*2 tablespoons butter*
$\frac{3}{4}$ tablespoon lemon juice	*$\frac{1}{4}$ cup sugar*
$1\frac{1}{2}$ egg whites (just below $\frac{1}{4}$ cup)	*$\frac{1}{4}$ cup boiling water*
	Pinch salt

1. Oil a 2-cup mould or 5 individual small ones.
2. Grate lemon rind. Squeeze juice. In a small bowl place lemon juice and cold water. Sprinkle gelatine into liquid and let stand.
3. Beat eggs, egg yolks, and sugar in a medium-sized bowl with an electric or rotary beater for 10 to 15 minutes. Mixture should about treble in volume.
4. Set bowl with gelatine in a pan of hot water over medium heat and stir to thoroughly dissolve gelatine. Mix slowly into egg mixture. Stir in lemon rind and whipped cream.

195

5. Pour into mould or moulds. Stir well and chill in refrigerator. After 30 minutes stir once more and chill until set, about 3 to 4 hours.

6. Prepare ORANGE DESSERT SAUCE while soufflé is chilling. Have juices ready before making. Beat egg whites until they are very stiff. Cream butter in a medium-sized bowl. Add sugar gradually and cream together. Place bowl over, but not in, hot water over low heat. Stir in boiling water and salt; mix until smooth. Add egg whites and juices at the same time and beat with a rotary or electric beater 2 to 3 minutes. Sauce will be foamy and light. Serve chilled. Stir or shake it before serving over soufflé.

The delicate orange sauce keeps 2 or 3 days refrigerated. It may also be used warm, and on other puddings. The dessert is good, too, with FROSTED ORANGE SECTIONS, without the orange sauce.

✄ FROSTED ORANGE SECTIONS

PREPARATION 15 MINUTES
DRYING 20 TO 40 MINUTES

| 2 *or* 3 *navel oranges* | *Granulated sugar* |
| 1 *egg white* | |

1. Peel oranges and remove as much white underskin as possible without piercing fruit. Divide oranges into sections.

2. Dip each section into unbeaten egg white and then into sugar. Be sure to coat sections all over with both. Place them on wax paper.

3. Before they are completely dry, dip sections in sugar once more. Let them dry.

4. Use when coating is stiff and looks frosty.

Small bunches of grapes may be treated in the same way.

196

✳ MERINGUE PUFFS ON LEMON WINE CUSTARD

SERVES 4 · PREPARATION: PUFFS—30 MINUTES
CUSTARD—10 MINUTES
CHILLING 4 HOURS

MERINGUE PUFFS

3 *cups water*	3 *egg whites*
A 2-*inch piece vanilla bean or*	3 *tablespoons sugar*
2 *teaspoons vanilla extract*	

LEMON WINE CUSTARD

5 *tablespoons water*	½ *cup sugar*
3 *tablespoons white wine*	1 *teaspoon grated lemon rind*
1½ *tablespoons lemon juice*	3 *egg yolks*

1. To make MERINGUE PUFFS use a large skillet or frying-pan. Boil water slowly with vanilla bean for 10 minutes. Remove bean. If using extract just bring water to boil and add it.

2. Have ready fresh dish towel on which to drain puffs. Beat egg whites as stiff as possible. Beat in sugar, 1 tablespoonful at a time. Wet a tablespoon with cold water and spoon up portion of meringue. Mould into small egg shape. Drop into gently boiling water. Poach for about 1½ minutes on each side or until puff is firm. Remove to towel. Cook a few at a time so as not to crowd pan. A collapsed puff indicates too long poaching. Cool puffs.

3. To make LEMON WINE CUSTARD, place water, wine, lemon juice, and sugar in a small pan. Heat just long enough to dissolve sugar. Add lemon rind. Remove from heat. Beat egg yolks slightly in a bowl and add 3 tablespoons of wine mixture, 1 tablespoon at a time, stirring. Return yolk-wine mixture to pan slowly and stir. Place directly over low heat. Keep stirring until mixture begins to thicken and coats spoon. This takes several minutes.

197

4. Remove custard from heat. Stir until it is cooled. The custard will thicken considerably when cool.

5. Serve custard well chilled with meringue puffs atop.

The French make *Oeufs sur Neige* (Eggs on Snow) which is similar but with the custard made with milk instead of wine. All water instead of water and wine may be used in this recipe.

✖ MOCHA PARFAIT PIE

SERVES 4 TO 5 · PREPARATION: CRUST 30 MINUTES,
FILLING 20 MINUTES
CHILLING SEVERAL HOURS

CHOCOLATE WAFER CRUMB CRUST

Chocolate wafers	4 *tablespoons butter*
1 *tablespoon sugar*	

MOCHA PARFAIT FILLING

4 *tablespoons butter, room temperature*	¼ *cup cold water*
1 *cup light brown sugar, well packed*	1 *cup water*
	2 *tablespoons instant coffee*
3 *egg yolks*	⅛ *teaspoon salt*
1½ *teaspoons unflavoured gelatine*	2 *tablespoons brandy or cognac*

1. To make CHOCOLATE WAFER CRUMB CRUST, crumble fine enough chocolate wafers to make ¾ cup of sieved crumbs. Sprinkle sugar over them. Melt butter and mix in well. Butter a 7-inch pie plate heavily. Spread crumb mixture over bottom and up sides of pan. Chill at least 20 minutes.

2. To make MOCHA PARFAIT FILLING, cream butter in a medium-sized bowl. Add sugar gradually and cream together until mixture is fluffy. Add unbeaten egg yolks and beat until mixture is smooth. An electric beater may be used for this step.

3. Sprinkle gelatine into cold water. Let it stand 5 minutes to

soften. Bring cup of water to boil. Turn off heat and stir in coffee and salt. Add gelatine and dissolve well. Stir into butter mixture with wooden spoon until it is smooth, or beat briefly with electric beater. Mix in brandy.

4. Chill filling, covered, until it is about to jell. Scrape sides of bowl and beat with a fork until filling is well blended but not foamy or bubbly. Chill it again until it is about to jell. Scrape and beat again. Chill a third time. Scrape and beat once more. Now spoon into prepared unbaked crust. Return pie to refrigerator and freeze until it is firm.

Prepare this the day before, if you wish. This dessert is just as good not frozen, but allowed to jell until firm. However, the gelatine must be increased to 2 teaspoons. Coffee lovers will enjoy the definite coffee flavour. An electric blender is perfect for crushing the wafers.

⅍ ZABAIONE

SERVES 3 · 15 TO 20 MINUTES

3 *egg yolks*   ½ *cup Marsala wine*
2½ *tablespoons sugar*

1. Have ready a little simmering water, about an inch high in the bottom of a double boiler. Keep over low heat.

2. Place egg yolks and sugar in a bowl and beat with an electric or rotary beater until eggs are pale yellow and have increased in volume, about 4 or 5 minutes. Add wine and mix.

3. Pour mixture into the top of a double boiler. Place it over simmering water that does not touch top pan. Beat constantly and rapidly with portable electric or rotary beater until mixture thickens and is fluffy, about 10 minutes.

4. Serve warm in sherbet glasses, or refrigerate and serve cold. A ladyfinger or a slice of sponge cake sometimes accompanies this dessert, but it is so rich that neither is necessary.

❧ Variation · FROZEN ZABAIONE

SERVES 3 · PREPARATION 18 TO 20 MINUTES
FREEZING 2 TO 3 HOURS

1. Use 3 tablespoons of sugar, and follow Steps 1, 2, 3. Let zabaione cool.
2. Thoroughly oil 3 small half-cup fluted or plain moulds. Turn them over to drain off excess oil.
3. Stir ½ cup whipped cream into cooled custard until it is well blended. Spoon it into moulds. Place in refrigerator to freeze 2 to 3 hours.

An unusual and fine dessert that can be whipped up in a few minutes. If necessary, it can be made a day ahead. I often serve it right in the moulds.

❧ WINE JELLY

SERVES 4 TO 6 · PREPARATION 15 MINUTES
CHILLING 2 TO 3 HOURS

⅓ cup orange juice
2 tablespoons lemon juice
1 tablespoon unflavoured
　gelatine
¼ cup cold water
½ cup boiling water
6 tablespoons sugar
Pinch salt
¾ cup port
¼ cup whipped cream
　(optional)

1. Strain juices.
2. Sprinkle gelatine on cold water to soften. Let stand 5 minutes.
3. Add boiling water and stir to dissolve gelatine thoroughly. Add sugar and salt; mix well. Add juices and port; stir; pour into moulds rinsed in cold water. Chill.
4. Serve chilled with 1 tablespoon of whipped cream if desired.

You can definitely taste the port in this jelly. If you like just a hint of port, reduce amount to ¼ cup, and increase orange juice to ½ cup and lemon juice to 3 tablespoons. Whipped cream adds a party touch to a robust jellied port. If you like port, you'll love this.

❧ RASPBERRY-PEACH SHERBET

SERVES 6 · PREPARATION 40 MINUTES EXCLUSIVE OF DEFROSTING
FREEZING 3 HOURS OR MORE

10 *ounces frozen raspberries*	¼ *cup heavy cream*
12 *ounces frozen peaches*	¼ *cup milk*
¼ *cup sugar*	2 *egg whites*
1 *tablespoon lemon juice*	*Pinch salt*

1. Defrost fruits. Drain off juices and save them. Push fruits through a food mill or strainer. Pour off juice that collects in purée and add it to other juices. Don't press purée to extract juice. There should be from ¾ to 1 cup of fruit.

2. Add enough water to juices to make 1½ cups of liquid. Stir in sugar and bring to a boil. Then cook slowly 10 minutes. Cool.

3. Put cooled syrup and purée through a fine strainer or cheesecloth-lined strainer to remove seeds. Stir in lemon juice. Chill. Pour into refrigerator ice tray. Set control at coldest position. Freeze mixture until it is firm at outer border and somewhat mushy in centre.

4. Turn it into a bowl. Beat about 2 minutes with an electric beater or a little longer with a hand beater, until mixture is light and creamy. Mix in cream and milk. Add salt to egg whites; beat them until they are very stiff, and fold them gently but thoroughly into mixture. Return to tray and freeze 1 hour.

5. Remove sherbet to bowl and beat as before. Return it to ice tray and freeze until it is firm. Then set control back to normal. For smoother sherbet, beat it for several seconds just before serving.

This may be made the day before, but beat it a little before serving to remove any iciness. The raspberry flavour predominates.

✄ TUTTI-FRUTTI FROZEN PUDDING

MAKES ONE QUART · PREPARATION 1 HOUR
STEEPING 3 HOURS OR OVERNIGHT ,
FREEZING SEVERAL HOURS

½ cup (4 ounces) candied cherries	1 cup sugar
	Pinch salt
½ cup (4 ounces) candied citron	2¼ cups milk
	2 eggs
¼ cup rum	1 cup whipping cream

1. Chop candied fruits coarsely or put through the coarse blade of a food chopper. Pour rum over fruit and let it steep, covered, 3 hours or overnight.

2. Add sugar and salt to milk in top of double boiler. Place over hot water and scald.

3. Beat eggs slightly a few seconds in large bowl. Pour hot milk mixture into bowl very slowly, stirring constantly.

4. Return to top of double boiler. Place over an inch of simmering water. Stir constantly with metal spoon until mixture begins to thicken. As soon as it coats spoon, remove from heat. This takes about 4 to 5 minutes. Be careful as egg mixtures curdle if cooked at too high temperature or too long.

5. Cool custard. Whip cream until stiff. Fold it thoroughly into custard. Add fruits with rum and pour into 2 refrigerator trays. Place in freezer or into freezing compartment of refrigerator set at highest freezing point. Let freeze 1 hour. Turn pudding into bowl and whip with an electric or hand beater until smooth and creamy.

6. Pour into individual glass dishes and finish freezing. Return cold control of refrigerator to normal.

This is best prepared a day ahead. Remove it from the refrigerator a few minutes before serving to thaw slightly if it has frozen too hard.

CHEESE, EGG, AND OTHER
LIGHT LUNCH DISHES

҂   ҂   ҂   ҂   ҂   ҂   ҂   ҂

THE recipe for pancakes, which is given here in the recipe for Cheese Blintzes, will be found valuable for its versatility. It can be put to use in a main dish or a dessert for either luncheon or dinner. Leftovers are glorified when they become fillings for the pancakes. Use minced, cooked chicken, turkey, beef, pork, shrimp, lobster, or crab meat, and combine with chopped celery, onion, toasted almonds, tarragon, parsley, etc. Moisten ingredients with a little sauce, gravy or cream to make a fine mixture. Filled, rolled, and crisped, the pancakes are attractive as well as tasty, whether or not they are served with a sauce such as Aurore, Mornay, or Curry. As a dessert, the pancakes can be filled with sweetened berries or other fruit to make a fine climax to a light dinner.

⊱ CHEESE BLINTZES

ABOUT 14 PANCAKES · 50 MINUTES

PANCAKE BATTER FOR
  BLINTZES

¾ *cup milk*
2 *eggs*
⅝ *cup flour, unsifted*
1–2 *tablespoons butter for*
  greasing

¼ *teaspoon salt*
2 *tablespoons sugar*

CHEESE FILLING

¾ *pound very dry cottage*
  cheese, room
  temperature
¼ *cup raisins* (optional)
2 to 3 *tablespoons butter*
½ *pint sour cream*

2 *egg yolks*
4 *tablespoons sugar*
½ *teaspoon vanilla or grated*
  orange rind

1. To make pancakes, place ingredients listed under Pancake Batter in a bowl. Beat them with an egg beater several seconds until they are fairly smooth.

2. Cover a cleared working surface, close to the range, with a dish towel or paper towels to receive turned out pancakes.

3. Heat a 6-inch frying-pan over moderate heat. When it is hot, grease bottom of pan with butter, using a brush or several folds of a paper towel. Pour into pan 1 large spoonful of batter. Work very quickly. Swirl batter to cover entire bottom. Pour off surplus batter. Let cook to pale brown, on under side, about 30 seconds. Cook on one side only.

4. Turn out on dish towel, cooked side up. Do not pile pancakes on top of each other. Place them side by side, overlapping slightly.

5. To make filling, mash cheese a little to soften it. Rinse raisins

204

in hot water to plump up. Squeeze them dry. Add with other ingredients to cheese and mix well.

6. Centre a large spoonful of cheese mixture on each pancake. Fold towards centre any 2 opposite sides. Start with third side, fold over pancake, like an envelope, to enclose filling completely.

7. Melt butter in a large frying-pan over moderate heat. When it is hot, place several blintzes, smooth side up, in pan and cook them until they are brown and crisp. Turn them with spatula and brown other side. Don't crowd them, or turning will be difficult. Keep blintzes warm until all are browned. Serve them with a bowl of chilled sour cream.

These may be made a day ahead and kept refrigerated. Just before serving, complete Step 7.

✻ CHEESE FONDUE

SERVES 3 TO 6 · 20 MINUTES

6 *slices white bread*   ½ *teaspoon salt*
6 *large eggs*   ⅛ *teaspoon white pepper*
¼ *pound Gruyère cheese*   *Dash cayenne*
1½ *tablespoons butter*

1. Toast bread and set it aside. Have hot serving plates ready.

2. Beat eggs in a bowl. Grate cheese into same bowl. Add butter cut into bits. Stir with wooden spoon until eggs and cheese are blended.

3. Pour into a skillet over a slow fire, and stir several minutes until mixture is thick and soft. Remove immediately. Season with salt, pepper, and cayenne.

4. Place toast on hot plates and spoon fondue on to toast.

For a solo snack or lunch, use 2 eggs, 1⅓ ounces of cheese (about 1 slice of Swiss cheese), ½ tablespoon of butter, and 2 slices of toast.

205

❧ HOME-MADE CREAM CHEESE

MAKES ¾ CUP TO 1 CUP · 2 TO 3 DAYS

1 quart fresh milk, non-homogenized

1. Heat milk in a saucepan slowly until lukewarm.
2. Rinse a glass quart jar with hot water. Pour milk into jar and cover it tightly.
3. Set it on a tile or plate on the pilot light of the gas range. The jar should feel lukewarm at all times. If it gets too warm, set it on a second tile or plate. Should adjacent burner be turned on high, move the jar to a less hot spot, as too rapid souring produces an undesirable taste. Let milk stand 24 to 48 hours. The solid part or curd will rise to the upper part of jar and the liquid will settle in lower half.
4. Set a sieve in a deep bowl. Line it with a large white napkin. Spoon solid curd into napkin. Discard liquid or whey. Gather ends of napkin together with a rubber band to form a bag. Squeeze it slightly to expel any liquid. Let it drain in refrigerator 24 hours. Pour off drained liquid occasionally.
5. Blend in 1 tablespoon of cream if desired. Serve cheese chilled.

These directions apply to cheese made at room temperature of about 70° F. If you do not have a stove with a pilot light, you might try setting the jar of milk with its tile(s) or plate(s) on a warm radiator, away from draughts, or on top of the furnace, but results will be unpredictable as an even and steady temperature is required. There are several ways of serving this cheese. Season it with salt and pepper and spread it on thin pumpernickel slices. Mix in chopped chives and spread it on plain crackers. For a light luncheon dish, serve it with sweetened sliced strawberries and pour a little cream round it. For dessert, mix it with slivered preserved ginger and serve over chilled stewed or tinned pear halves.

⅍ PUFFY CHEESE TOAST

SERVES 2 · 15 MINUTES

¼ *pound cheese,* ⅔ *of it*   ½ *teaspoon salt*
   Cheddar, ⅓ *Swiss*   ⅛ *teaspoon pepper*
1 *large egg*   *Few grains cayenne*
1½ *tablespoons milk*   2 *slices white bread, crusts on*
1½ *tablespoons flour*

1. Heat slowly a pot of deep oil or fat to about 350°.

2. Grate enough cheese to make 1 cupful.

3. Combine egg, milk, flour, salt, pepper, and cayenne. Add cheese and mix. Batter should be very thick. Spread half of it over one side of each slice of bread.

4. Drop bread, cheese side down, into hot fat. Let it cook until top of bread toasts brown. The underside will be puffy, crisp, crusty, and cinnamon-coloured, with a soft, creamy interior. Drain toast on unglazed paper or paper towels. Serve at once.

An excellent luncheon or supper dish. You may use all Cheddar cheese instead of the suggested combination, or equal parts of Cheddar, Swiss, and Muenster. Serve with sliced tomato on lettuce shreds with FRENCH DRESSING and olives.

⅍ WELSH RAREBIT ON TOAST

SERVES 1 OR 2 · 8 MINUTES

2 *slices white bread*   2 *teaspoons brandy, ale, or*
⅔ *cup diced sharp Cheddar*   *port*
   cheese   *Tiny pinch cayenne*

1. Toast bread. (Butter it if you wish.)

2. Cut cheese into small dice. Warm a small heavy pan over medium heat. Place cheese in it with brandy, ale, or port. Stir with a fork until cheese has almost melted, a minute or two.

3. Pour cheese over toast. Sprinkle it with cayenne. Eat it while it is hot.

Tasty and quick for that moment when you'd like just a little something to eat.

✂ FRENCH OMELET

SERVES 1 · 3 TO 4 MINUTES

2 eggs	*Pinch pepper*
½ *teaspoon cold water*	*Scant tablespoon of butter*
⅛ *teaspoon salt*	

1. Combine all ingredients except butter in a bowl. Beat them with an egg beater about 15 seconds.

2. Place an 8-inch frying-pan with butter over moderate heat. Let butter melt. When it is about to brown, pour in eggs. Take time to scrape all egg from bowl. This allows time for eggs to coagulate at bottom. Shake pan a few seconds until egg has cooked into a thin pancake on the bottom. Then with a fork, gently so as not to tear it, keep stirring liquid egg until it thickens to the consistency of sour cream and 2 or 3 tablespoonfuls of egg are left. With a spatula or knife or both, fold edges of omelet over quickly to form an elliptical shape. Turn heat off, and slide omelet on to plate. It will finish cooking on the plate.

3. If it is to be filled, add filling just before folding omelet.

A pan used exclusively for omelets is a must for a well-made omelet. Get a cast-iron pan, keep it out of water, and clean it with a paper towel. If you follow these instructions, a minimum of butter will be required and your omelets won't stick. As for fillings, they are innumerable. As a rule, the ingredients (except for herbs) should be minced or chopped and sautéed first. Use mushrooms, chicken liver, ham, bacon, onion, spinach, tomato, sausage, asparagus, etc., alone or in combination.

⚹ WESTERN FINES HERBES OMELET

SERVES 2 · 15 MINUTES

3 *tablespoons cooked ham*	2 *tablespoons chopped*
3 *tablespoons onion*	*parsley*
3 *tablespoons green pepper*	2 *tablespoons butter*
2 *scallions with tops*	4 *eggs*
(optional)	$\frac{1}{4}$ *teaspoon salt*
1 *small tomato*	*Dash Tabasco or* $\frac{1}{8}$
2 *tablespoons chopped fresh*	*teaspoon pepper*
dill	1$\frac{1}{2}$ *tablespoons butter*

1. Mince ham and vegetables. Chop dill and parsley.
2. Melt butter in a small pan over moderate heat. Cook ham and vegetables for 5 minutes.
3. Beat eggs well. Stir in herbs, salt, and Tabasco or pepper. Melt butter in a 10-inch skillet over moderate heat. Pour in eggs and cook until they are firm but still a little moist in the centre. See FRENCH OMELET. Spoon two-thirds of sautéed mixture over half of omelet. Fold over to cover filling. Divide omelet in two. Serve on heated plates, garnished with remaining third of mixture.

Good with pumpernickel.

✂ EGGS FOO YONG

SERVES 2 TO 4 · 30 MINUTES

½ cup chopped mushrooms
3 scallions with tops
¼ cup onions
½ cup celery
¼ cup leftover cooked
vegetable

½ cup cooked meat, shrimp,
or crab
2 tablespoons bland oil
½ cup bean sprouts
1 tablespoon soy sauce

CHINESE BROWN SAUCE

1 teaspoon cornflour
¼ teaspoon dry mustard

2 teaspoons soy sauce
½ cup chicken broth or water

4 eggs, well beaten
¼ teaspoon salt

⅛ teaspoon pepper

1. Chop mushrooms. Mince scallions and onion. Slice celery thinly. Mince cooked vegetable and meat or fish.

2. Heat oil in a medium-sized skillet over medium heat. Sauté mushrooms for 2 minutes. Add and cook scallions, onions, and celery for 2 minutes. Add cooked vegetable, meat or fish, bean sprouts, and soy sauce. Mix. Cook 1 minute. Turn off heat.

3. To make CHINESE BROWN SAUCE, blend cornflour, mustard, and soy sauce until smooth. Add broth or water. Stir and let simmer for a few minutes.

4. While sauce simmers, make an omelet. Beat eggs well. Season them with salt and pepper. Add contents of skillet and mix. Brush well with a little oil the bottom of a 6-inch frying-pan. Turn heat to moderate. When pan is hot, drop in a large spoonful of egg mixture. Spread it all over the bottom. Cook as you would a pancake. Flip it over when it is medium brown. Brown other side. Grease pan again for each pancake; this recipe makes 4.

5. Pour sauce over omelet and serve at once.

Any kind of meat or shellfish may be used. Bean sprouts are not absolutely essential. If they are not available, just increase the amount of some other vegetable used. Served with BOILED RICE and BUTTERED CABBAGE, this dish makes a substantial luncheon or supper.

⅍ POACHED EGGS WITH ONIONS ON TOAST

SERVES 2 TO 4 · 10 MINUTES

1 *medium-sized onion*	*Freshly ground black pepper*
4 *eggs*	1 *teaspoon chopped parsley*
Garlic salt	4 *slices white bread*
Celery salt	

1. Use an egg poacher. Grease insides of cups well. Place them in poacher with enough water to cover lower half of cups.
2. Slice onion thinly and separate it into rings. Divide them among the 4 cups. Drop an egg gently into each cup. Sprinkle it with seasonings to taste. Top with chopped parsley. Bring water to a boil. Cover pan and let eggs steam for 3 to 4 minutes until a film forms over the yolks and the whites are firm. Test with a knife for desired firmness.
3. While eggs poach, toast bread and butter it.
4. If necessary, use a knife to loosen eggs from cups. Serve eggs on hot buttered toast.

⅍ FRENCH WINE TOAST

MAKES 1 SLICE OF TOAST · 10 MINUTES

3 *tablespoons sauterne or any*	½ *tablespoon butter*
sweet white wine	1 *slice white bread*
1 *tablespoon sugar*	*Sugar for sprinkling*
1 *egg yolk*	*Cinnamon (optional)*
Good pinch salt	

211

1. Mix sugar and wine. Add salt to egg yolk and beat.
2. Melt butter slowly in a pan.
3. Dip bread quickly into wine to moisten it. Wine will be absorbed. Then dip bread into egg yolk.
4. Place bread in pan; raise heat to moderately high and brown on both sides until somewhat crisp.
5. Sprinkle toast with sugar, with or without a sprinkling of cinnamon, and eat it while it is hot.

⅍ MATZO MEAL PANCAKES

6 PANCAKES · 15 MINUTES

SOUR CREAM TOPPING

½ *cup sour cream*	*Grated rind* ½ *lemon*
1 *tablespoon sugar*	

2 *eggs, separated*	⅓ *cup milk or water*
⅓ *cup matzo meal*	½ *teaspoon salt*

1. To make SOUR CREAM TOPPING, grate lemon rind and mix with sour cream and sugar. Set aside until it is needed.
2. Beat egg yolks well. Add and mix matzo meal, milk or water. and salt. Batter will be thick.
3. Beat whites until they are very stiff. Fold them into batter.
4. Heat a griddle and grease it well. Drop batter from a wooden spoon on to griddle. Cook over medium heat until pancake is brown. Turn and brown second side. Grease griddle for each batch.
5. Serve pancakes hot with a spoonful of topping over each pancake.

The pancakes are feather-light, the topping simple and delectable. Good for breakfast or luncheon.

⅍ SOUR CREAM PANCAKES

MAKES ABOUT 10 SMALL PANCAKES · 25 MINUTES

½ cup large-curd cottage
   cheese
2 eggs
¾ cup sour cream

¾ cup unsifted flour
½ teaspoon baking soda
1 teaspoon salt
Sugar for sprinkling

1. Press cheese through a sieve into a bowl.

2. Beat eggs and blend into cheese. Stir in sour cream.

3. Sift together flour, baking soda, and salt. Add to cheese mixture. Beat thoroughly. Let stand 5 to 10 minutes.

4. Heat a griddle. Grease it. Drop batter from a wooden spoon and cook pancakes over medium heat until they are brown on both sides.

5. Sprinkle pancakes with sugar and eat them while they are hot. They can be served with the very good SOUR CREAM TOPPING (see MATZO MEAL PANCAKES).

BRIEFLY: BREADS

✂ ✂ ✂ ✂ ✂ ✂ ✂ ✂

UNBLEACHED flour and large eggs should be used in these recipes.

I am especially proud of my recipe for "stove-top" scones. There are literally dozens upon dozens of recipes for scones, but most of them call for oven baking. Treacle, bridge, oatmeal, potato pancake, fruit, and syrup scones are just a few favourites.

The English muffins may be made with any white bread dough.

✂ BOSTON BROWN BREAD
SERVES 6 TO 10 · 2½ TO 2¾ HOURS

2 cups sour milk
⅔ cup molasses
3 cups Boston brown bread meal or 1 cup yellow water-ground corn meal, 1 cup rye flour, and 1 cup graham flour

2 teaspoons baking soda
1 teaspoon salt
½ cup moist raisins
2 tablespoons melted butter

1. Grease all over with bland oil the insides of 3 medium tins or 4 slightly smaller ones. Invert them on a plate to drain off

214

excess oil. Place a rack or trivet in a large pot and fill it with enough water to come halfway up sides of tins. Heat water until it boils.

2. Mix together sour milk and molasses. Sift into these liquids the meal, soda, and salt. Add raisins. Mix all together until flour is well dampened. Stir in butter.

3. Fill greased moulds ⅔ full of batter. Cover moulds snugly with 4 thicknesses of aluminium foil. Set them on rack in pot. Bring water rapidly to a boil; cover and reduce heat. Steam bread over very low heat 2¼ to 2½ hours. If water falls below half-way level, add some boiling water. Bread should be moist but firm when done.

4. Remove tins from pot. Run knife all around bread. Turn bread out on to a rack to cool. Wrap it in waxed paper and then in foil if it is not to be used the same day.

The Boston brown bread meal can be purchased in 2-pound bags at health food stores. Fresh milk can be easily converted to sour milk by mixing 3 tablespoons of white vinegar into 2 cups of lukewarm milk, but be sure milk is no warmer than tepid or it will curdle too much. Let it stand 10 minutes before you use it. If raisins are dry, drop them into a little hot water for 15 seconds and drain them; squeeze out gently any water in raisins. The bread of course goes with baked beans. When it is spread with butter, cream cheese, and chopped nuts, it makes a fine sandwich for lunch or tea.

CRUMPETS

MAKES ABOUT ONE DOZEN · 25 MINUTES

2 cups all-purpose flour	¼ teaspoon baking soda
2 tablespoons butter	2 eggs, unbeaten
2 teaspoons sugar	¾ cup milk
¼ teaspoon cream of tartar	

1. Place flour in a bowl. Cut butter in with a pastry blender or 2 knives.

2. Add dry ingredients and mix well.

3. Make a well in centre of batter. Drop in eggs and ¼ cup milk. Beat vigorously but quickly with a wooden spoon for a few seconds. Add remainder of milk and mix with a few strokes. Batter will be thick and lumpy.

4. Heat a griddle slowly. When it is hot, brush it with oil. Turn heat to medium. Drop batter with a wooden spoon on to greased griddle and cook about 3 minutes until 3 or 4 bubbles break and underside of crumpet is cinnamon-coloured. Turn and cook other side, about 2 minutes, until it is brown. Griddle may need to be greased to bake the second side.

5. Serve crumpets warm and spread with butter.

✂ SCOTCH DROPPED SCONES

MAKES ABOUT 10 SCONES · 25 MINUTES

2 *cups unsifted flour*	½ *tablespoon sugar*
1 *teaspoon baking soda*	1 *egg*
1 *teaspoon cream of tartar*	1 *cup buttermilk*
¼ *teaspoon salt*	*Small piece suet or a little oil*

1. Heat a griddle over medium heat until it is hot.

2. Sift dry ingredients in a medium-sized bowl.

3. Beat egg well. Pour half of it into a small bowl. (The remaining half will not be needed.) Add buttermilk and stir until well blended. Use a wooden spoon and mix into flour quickly with a few swift, light strokes. The less the batter is handled at this point, the better the result. The batter should be very thick, almost thick enough to be rolled out. When dropped from a spoon it should fall heavily with little help.

4. Grease a griddle with suet or bland oil. Using a wooden spoon three-quarters full, drop batter on to griddle. Scones should be half an inch apart. Cook them about 3 or 4 minutes until they are medium brown. Turn and cook the other side 3 or 4 minutes. Touch sides of scones; they should be dryish when they are done.

5. Serve scones hot. Pull them apart and butter them.

These scones are fine for breakfast. They look like muffins and taste somewhat like them too. They are easy to make. When cold, they may be pulled apart and toasted on the inside.

✄ MUFFINS

MAKES 12 TO 14 THREE-INCH MUFFINS · PREPARATION
25 MINUTES
RISING ABOUT 3 HOURS
BAKING 15 TO 20 MINUTES

½ *cup water*	1¼ *teaspoons salt*
1 *packet dry yeast or 1*	1 *tablespoon sugar*
cake compressed yeast	3 *cups sifted unbleached*
½ *cup milk*	*flour*
2 *tablespoons butter*	2 *tablespoons corn meal*

1. Sprinkle dry yeast into warm water, 105–115° F. (A few drops on the inside of your wrist should feel very warm, but not hot.) Or crumble yeast cake into lukewarm water, 80–85° F. (Water tested on the wrist will feel neither warm nor cold.) Stir mixture until yeast is dissolved.

2. Scald milk. Drop into it butter, cut into bits, salt, and sugar. Stir until butter is melted and combined with milk. Cool to lukewarm.

3. Add yeast to milk mixture and mix well.

217

4. Sift flour and reserve $\frac{1}{4}$ cup. Add half of remaining flour to milk mixture and stir with a wooden spoon until blended. Add the other half and beat until flour is absorbed into dough. Dough will be sticky.

5. Use a little of the reserved flour to dust a board or pastry cloth. Place dough on floured surface and knead about 7 or 8 minutes, adding a little reserved flour if the dough is too sticky to handle. Dough should lose its stickiness and become smooth and elastic. Try to keep it soft by using as little of the extra flour as possible.

6. Grease a large bowl. Turn ball of dough in it to grease, and cover dough lightly with a dish towel. Set it in a sunny location or in a warm place away from draughts, 85–90° F., and let dough rise until it almost triples in bulk. Plunge 2 fingers into dough; if impression remains, it is ready for rolling.

7. Place dough on floured surface. Knead it a few seconds to round up. Roll it out to $\frac{1}{2}$-inch thickness. Cut dough into rounds, 3 to $3\frac{3}{4}$ inches in diameter. Sprinkle a baking sheet with corn meal. Lift rounds with spatula into muffin rings or on to sheet, spaced an inch or so apart. Cover and let them rise in a warm place, until they are light, about an hour.

8. Heat an ungreased griddle over low heat until it is hot, about 10 minutes. Set muffins on griddle, well spaced, to allow for further rising. Sprinkle tops with a few grains of corn meal. Bake 7 to 10 minutes, or until bottom is light brown; sides will not brown. Turn and brown other side, baking about the same time. If heat is uneven, shift muffins about when some are done.

9. Remove muffins to a rack to cool. Store them in wax paper.

10. To serve, split muffins apart with fingers, and toast and butter them.

For a professional product, it is nice to bake these in muffin rings. I bake mine in $3\frac{3}{4}$-inch moulds for shaping hamburgers, without the metal bottom disc. Perfectly satisfactory muffins can be made with no moulds at all. Please don't be afraid of this recipe; though it looks complicated, it is not. I have used a lot of words to make sure that even a novice at yeast baking can achieve success. You can double the recipe, except for yeast and sugar and butter, to use for oven-baked bread.

⚜ KITCHEN TECHNIQUES

BASTE: Moisten food by spooning over it fat or other liquid.

BLEND: Mix ingredients thoroughly so that separate ingredients are not distinguishable.

BRAISE: Cook by browning food in hot fat first, then complete cooking in a small amount of liquid.

COAT: Cover foods with dry or liquid ingredients as flour, egg, breadcrumbs.

CREAM: Work butter or lard or margarine with back of spoon or rubber scraper until it is soft, smooth, and creamy. Or use electric mixer.

CUBE: Cut into small-sized particles as for chicken salad.

DEVEIN SHRIMP: Start near feet and strip off shell. With a small knife, make a shallow slit at top side from head to tail. Remove black intestinal vein.

DICE: Cut into small cubes.

DUST: Sprinkle lightly with dry ingredients such as spices, herbs, flour, etc.

FLAME WITH BRANDY: Measure required amount of brandy into a spoon or small dish. (Remove brandy bottle from cooking area.) Pour brandy over hot ingredients, light a match, and touch it to brandy-moistened food. When flames begin to die down, cover food for a few moments to keep the aroma from dissipating.

FLUFF: Use 2 forks to lift up gently and loosen mixture.

FOLD: Slip rubber scraper or spoon gently down side or centre of bowl to the bottom. With a vertical motion, move scraper upwards, folding lifted food to top. Repeat straight down, under, and straight up motions until mixture is well blended. This method of mixing is used to prevent enclosed air from escaping.

GRATE LEMON OR ORANGE PEEL: Use a fine grater and grate peel on to waxed paper. Store grated peel, folded in the paper, if it is not to be used immediately.

HARD-BOIL EGGS: Place eggs in a large amount of cold water and bring to a boil. Remove from heat and let them stand, covered, 20 minutes.

KNEAD: Work and press dough with palms, heels, and knuckles of hands in a rhythmic motion. Dough is usually kneaded until it is smooth and loses its stickiness.

MAKE TOAST FINGERS, TRIANGLES, SQUARES: Toast lightly white bread slices, crusts removed. Cut toast into thirds lengthwise for fingers, diagonally in half for triangles, into four parts for squares.

MINCE: Cut or chop into fine small bits.

PARBOIL: Cook food partially in boiling water, anywhere from two minutes to a third or a half of the normal cooking time, depending upon the recipe. Cooking of parboiled food is completed by another method.

PLUMP UP RAISINS: Place in hot water one-half minute. Drain and squeeze out water gently. Dry.

POACH: Cook in simmering liquid, so as to keep the shape and flavour of food intact.

PREPARE AVOCADO PEAR: Avocado pears spoil rapidly, so prepare just before using. To keep fruit from discolouring, sprinkle it all over with lemon juice after it is cut. Remove stone.

PREPARE BREADCRUMBS: Make fresh breadcrumbs by powdering day-old bread with fingers. Make fine breadcrumbs by crumbling or grating dry or toasted bread, or use the packaged variety.

PREPARE NUTS: Blanch by dropping shelled nuts into rapidly boiling water. Remove from heat and let stand 1 minute. Drain, slip off skins with fingers, and let nuts dry on paper towels. Sliver almonds by splitting them in halves and cutting them into long thin shreds. Toast whole, halved, or slivered blanched almonds by sautéing in a hot pan with a little oil, about ½ teaspoon to ½ cup of nuts. Stir occasionally to prevent burning. Brown lightly. For toasted chopped almonds, sauté whole or halved blanched almonds; then chop. Toast other nuts the same way. For sliced hazelnuts, blanch, slice, and sauté.

PREPARE STRAWBERRIES: Keep in basket or place in strainer and rinse berries under cold running water 2 or 3 times. Remove green stems. Let drain. Do not wash berries until you are ready to use them.

PREPARE QUICK CHICKEN OR BEEF BROTH: Dissolve 1 chicken or beef bouillon cube in a cup of boiling water.

PURÉE FOODS: Press foods through sieve, food mill, or turn into electric blender.

REDUCE LIQUIDS: Boil rapidly and uncovered until amount of liquid has been reduced to specified quantity.

REMOVE FAT FROM BROTH OR SAUCES: Chill liquid in refrigerator. Remove congealed layer of fat. Or set container of liquid in a deep pan of cold water. Keep water cold. Remove fat that floats to the top.

SAUTÉ: Cook food in shallow fat. (This is also called pan frying.)

SCALD MILK: Heat milk to just the boiling point.

SIEVE: Press through sieve or food mill.

SIMMER: Cook in hot water just below the boiling point. At simmering point, very small bubbles rise to the surface and break.

SKIN PEACHES: Put fruit into boiling water. Let stand ½ minute. Remove peaches and peel off skins.

SKIN TOMATOES: Use above method. Or impale stem end on a fork and rotate over medium heat of burner until skin blisters and darkens. Peel skin off with a knife.

UNMOULD A DISH: Slip knife carefully down sides. Invert mould over a platter, tapping the mould lightly. Or brush bottom of mould with warm moistened cloth and turn out.

WHISK: Beat or whip lightly in quick strokes, especially with the aid of a wire beater called a whisk.

INDEX